CREATING A
JAPANESE GARDEN

CREATING A
JAPANESE GARDEN

A step-by-step guide to pond, dry, tea, stroll and courtyard gardens

Practical advice, projects and plant directory, with over 270 photographs

Charles Chesshire

Special photography by Alex Ramsay

southwater

This edition is published by Southwater
an imprint of Anness Publishing Ltd,
Blaby Road, Wigston,
Leicestershire LE18 4SE

info@anness.com;
www.hermeshouse.com;
www.annesspublishing.com

If you like the images in this book and would
like to investigate using them for publishing,
promotions or advertising, please visit our
website www.practicalpictures.com for
more information.

Publisher: Joanna Lorenz
Editorial Director: Helen Sudell
Project Editors: Emma Clegg and
  Hannah Consterdine
Designers: Simon Daley and Mike Morey
Jacket design: Andrew Barron
Illustrators: Anna Koska and Anna Laflin
Special photography: Alex Ramsay
Production Controller: Bessie Bai

Previously published as part of a larger volume,
A Practical Guide to Japanese Gardening

ETHICAL TRADING POLICY
At Anness Publishing we believe that business
should be conducted in an ethical and
ecologically sustainable way, with respect for
the environment and a proper regard to the
replacement of the natural resources we employ.

As a publisher, we use a lot of wood pulp in
high-quality paper for printing, and that wood
commonly comes from spruce trees. We are
therefore currently growing more than 750,000
trees in three Scottish forest plantations:
Berrymoss (130 hectares/320 acres), West
Touxhill (125 hectares/305 acres) and Deveron
Forest (75 hectares/185 acres). The forests we
manage contain more than 3.5 times the
number of trees employed each year in making
paper for the books we manufacture.

Because of this ongoing ecological investment
programme, you, as our customer, can have the
pleasure and reassurance of knowing that a tree
is being cultivated on your behalf to naturally
replace the materials used to make the book
you are holding.

Our forestry programme is run in accordance
with the UK Woodland Assurance Scheme
(UKWAS) and will be certified by the
internationally recognized Forest Stewardship
Council (FSC). The FSC is a non-government
organization dedicated to promoting responsible
management of the world's forests. Certification
ensures forests are managed in an
environmentally sustainable and socially
responsible way. For further information about this
scheme, go to www.annesspublishing.com/trees

PUBLISHER'S NOTE
Although the advice and information in this
book are believed to be accurate and true at the
time of going to press, neither the authors nor
the publisher can accept any legal responsibility
or liability for any errors or omissions that may
have been made nor for any inaccuracies nor for
any loss, harm or injury that comes about from
following instructions or advice in this book.

PUBLISHER'S ACKNOWLEDGEMENTS
The publisher would like to thank the following for
kindly allowing photography to take place in their
gardens: Stella Hore of the Japanese Garden and
Bonsai Nursery, St Mawgan, Cornwall; Frances
Rasch at Heale Garden and Plant Centre,
Salisbury, Wiltshire; the Japanese-style roof,
Brunei Gallery, School of Oriental and African
Studies, London; the Royal Botanic Gardens in
Kew, London; Newstead Abbey, Newstead Abbey
Park, Nottinghamshire; the Pureland Zen Garden,
Nottinghamshire; the Tully Japanese Garden,
courtesy of The Irish National Stud Co., Tully, Co.
Kildare, Ireland; Helmut Kern at Stadt Karlsruhe,
Karlsruhe, Germany; Stadt Augsburg (Augsburg
Botanic Garden) in Germany; the Bonn Japanese
Garden in Rheinaue Park, Nordrhein-Westfalen,
Germany; Lisa Blackburn at The Huntington
Library, Art Collections and Botanical Gardens,
San Marino CA 91108; Kazuo Tamura of
Tatsumura Silk Company for his garden of Syoko-
ho-en; and to the other temples and gardens in
Japan who kindly gave us permission to take
photographs: Byodo-in, Hakusa sonso, the Heian
Shrine, Honen-in, Isui-en, Kinkaku-ji, Koetsu-ji,
Konchi-in, Koto-in, Murin-an, Nanzen-ji, Nigo
Caste, Ryogen-in, Sanzen-in, Shoden-ji, Tenju-an,
Tofuku-Ji and Toji-in.

The majority of photographs in this book were
taken by Alex Ramsay. A selection were also
provided from Charles Chesshire's collection.
Thanks also to Peter Busby, who very kindly gave
us access to the late Maureen Busby's extensive
photographic record of garden projects.

All photographs are © Anness Publishing Ltd
unless stated otherwise.

The publisher would like to thank the following
agencies and individuals for allowing their
photographs to be reproduced:
(t = top; b = bottom; c = centre; r = right; l = left)
Alamy Images: p51b (Juniors Bildarchiv), 59b
(Andrew Holt), p60t (Aflo Co. Ltd), p74t (Simon
Colmer and Abby Rex) Peter Busby: p22t;
Charles Chesshire: p36t, p46t, p59t, p71br,
p74m, p74b, p75b, p77bl, p78bl, p79bl,
p80bl, p83tr, p85bl; Corbis: p73tl (Mark
Bolton); Tadashi Kajiyana p72bl, p76tr.

Page 1: *A dramatically pruned pine at Kew
Gardens, London, UK*
Page 2: *Ilex crenata*
Page 3, from left: *A tea garden; Hydrangea; a
valley-style lantern at Pureland Zen gardens, UK*
Page 4, from top: *A pond garden; Acer
palmatum; stepping stones in a bed of moss; a
Chinese-style red-painting bridge at the Tully
Japanese Garden in Ireland; Prunus x yedoensis*
Page 5, from left: *A water basin and fountain
typical of those found in tea gardens; a stream
winding through a stroll garden*

Contents

Introduction

The Japanese garden has captured the imagination of Western gardeners ever since they discovered its delights in the 19th century. Japan, isolated from the rest of the world from the 1630s for over 200 years, had been nurturing extraordinary and unique styles of architecture, poetry, painting, flower arranging and gardening. When artists, architects and designers from the West were finally exposed to these Japanese arts in the late 19th century, they were astonished by what they found, and the strong influence of Japanese arts is still being felt today. Of these arts, Japanese garden design in particular exerts a powerful and mystical grip. Steeped in significance and refinement, the Japanese garden has enormous appeal, especially for garden designers seeking both a deeper meaning and a more contemporary edge.

Above: *Dry rock arrangements are often centred around a main stone which may represent the Buddha or Mount Horai of the Mystic Isles.*

THE STYLES OF JAPANESE GARDEN

Japanese landscape gardens can be broken down into five main styles – pond, dry, tea, stroll and courtyard – and each of these has a long and intimate relationship with the history of Japan. Even a modest knowledge of Japanese history, especially the country's relationship with China and Buddhism, will go a long way towards helping us to understand the art of the Japanese garden, and thereby enable us to reproduce it.

It was the dynamic, creative energies of Zen monks and painters of the medieval period that set the stage for the development of the unique art form that is the Japanese garden.

These ancient gardens, especially those constructed of stone and sand (some of which survive even from the 15th century), have become the benchmark of abstract garden art throughout the world.

KEY FEATURES

Water is one of the most important elements in the Japanese garden. It can often be found in the form of a pond, a stream or a simple small water basin. Even when water is absent, its presence is often suggested through areas of sand and gravel, or dry streams.

Rocks are equally significant features and are considered to possess a kind of spiritual and living essence that needs to be respected if they are to be placed successfully.

An understanding of the two elements of rock and water, through careful observation in nature, will

Left: *This ambitious waterfall scheme in the Rheinaue Garden in Germany creates drama through well-observed rock arrangements and in the way that the water spills over the rocks.*

help to form a good basis for creating Japanese-style gardens. The more you appreciate the natural law of these elements, the better the effect when used in the design of your garden.

HOW TO USE THIS BOOK

This book shows you how to create a beautiful and individual Japanese garden by using and adapting elements of the five classic styles, whether you want to plan a small garden in its entirety, or focus on a specific area in a more spacious area.

The chapters look at the five main garden types in turn – pond gardens, dry gardens, tea gardens, stroll gardens and courtyard gardens. Each section explains the style, first outlining key features, and then presenting a design proposal for a garden of that type. Three practical sequences showing the typical stages for each one show you how to bring the design to fruition. Some of the features, such as constructing a pine island, involve detailed planning and logistics; others, such as setting a lantern or laying a paving stone path, are relatively simple. They can all be adapted to the requirements of individual schemes, and many can be used within other garden styles.

HOW TO USE THE PLANT DIRECTORY

Plants are fundamental to all but a few Japanese gardens. Most of the plants used possess symbolic significance, including the twisted pine, scattered cherry blossom, pendulous wisteria, the lotus ('purity rising out of the mud') and fiery Japanese maple. The final chapter in this book surveys the plants, flowers and trees that you can use in your garden, laid out in an easy-to-use directory, illustrated with photographs of the most commonly used plants.

Within the directory, the plants are split into sections relating to seasons and particular types, including spring trees and shrubs, summer flowers, autumn foliage and evergreen shrubs. Each entry within these sections features the botanical name, the Japanese name, the common name and the plant's family. This is followed by a general introduction to that genus with a description of the plant that covers its leaves, flowers and growth habit. There are also brief notes on methods of propagation, flowering time, average size, preferred conditions, as well as a guide to the plant's hardiness, which is explained more fully at the end of the book.

POND GARDENS

Ponds, lakes and streams are central to the Japanese garden, instilling a sense of tranquillity, joy and calm. Water features, such as ponds and streams, always appear totally natural within the surrounding landscape, even if they are constructed artificially, and often avoid features or artefacts that are obviously manmade.

The Sakuteiki, which was written in Heian times, names many forms of pond styles, islands, streams and waterfalls, and even notes the best techniques for planting trees. Even now, we can draw on this ancient work for inspiration when designing contemporary pond gardens. For example, when placing rocks or choosing the course of a stream, you need to follow the "desire" or "request" of the stone or water.

The pond or lake, which is the central feature of the garden should be large enough for a small boat and there should be at least one island in the pond. These islands, often linked by bridges, can be planted with pine trees or grasses to create a natural scene. The outline of the pond itself can be indented with coves, beaches and grottoes, with the land around the pond made up of hills planted naturalistically with groups of trees.

Above: *Short and stocky lanterns are often placed near water or at the end of gravel spits to evoke lighthouses.*
Left: *A turtle island in Huntingdon Botanical Gardens, Los Angeles.*

The pond garden style

Starting with the very earliest gardens influenced by the Chinese and developing over the centuries to the most up-to-date designs, pond gardens have always been enormously popular in Japan. The pond will, naturally, be the central feature, and should ideally be big enough for you to incorporate an island or two, and, for greater authenticity, to make a ride in a small rowing boat possible. For this you will need space – it is obviously not suitable for a small town garden – as well as the time and energy to plan on a large scale.

ELEMENTS OF A POND GARDEN

The pond gardens of Japan were originally found only in city complexes. Despite being surrounded by buildings, these gardens were very naturalistic and much less stylized than the later stroll gardens. Ponds (with pine islands) and streams are the main features, along with naturalistic planting and a strolling path.

Pond

The edges of the pond should have a varied and natural outline resembling a coastline, with coves, grotto-like caves and beaches. Rocks can be placed at the edges of ponds and by waterfalls so long as their shape is considered carefully, and also in the water, where they can be used as stepping stones or supports for naturalistic bridges.

Above: *At the Heian shrine, in Kyoto, the staggered stepping stones are made of recycled bridge piers and temple column bases. Borrowing old architectural fragments is known as* mitate *("to see anew").*

Below: *Chinese-style red-painted bridges, such as this one at the Tully Japanese Garden in Ireland, were popular in the early days of Japanese gardens of the Heian period. They were also used extensively in later Edo gardens and copied in Western versions.*

Island

There are many styles of island to choose from, but the most popular is the pine island, planted with one very picturesque pine, or a group of pines set in a tight group. In pond gardens the island is often reached by a bridge, especially an old-style Chinese wooden bridge that is painted red or orange. You may of course prefer a different style of bridge, perhaps aiming for a more minimal, neutral effect.

Stream

Another main feature of a pond garden is a winding stream that either feeds into or empties the main pond (or both). This would originally have been used for ceremonial purposes, but even without the ceremonies it makes an attractive addition. Again it should follow a naturalistic course, and be planted at its edges with hostas and other waterside plants.

Plants

Planting in pond gardens should be in naturalistic groups of trees and shrubs that celebrate the seasons. Groves of cherries, maples and pines can be underplanted with azaleas, kerria and spiraea for contrast.

Path

A strolling path is the final essential feature that should be added, in order to encourage the visitor to experience every part of the garden by wandering around the pond, over the stream and through the groves of trees.

Above left: *A valley-style lantern, typical of the type used to arc over the edges of ponds at Pureland Zen garden, England.*

Above right: *Stepping stone paths that continue across ponds help to create a unity of design within a garden.*

Below: *The use of large rocks and clipped evergreens gives this pond garden a sense of scale that is much larger than in reality. The waterfall design carefully observes the natural flow of mountain streams.*

How to make a pond garden

Pond gardens do not necessarily require a spectacular country setting. They were originally made in Japanese cities in large walled spaces, which means that the pond garden is a style that can easily be reproduced in Western gardens. However, a minimum of a quarter of a hectare (over half an acre) is required to make the style effective. Here is a suggestion for a pond garden created with a clay-lined pond, a pine island and a waterfall, all of which are key elements of the style. On the next few pages follow practical sequences on each of these three elements, with instructions on how to prepare and install them. This will give a good foundation plan for creating a pond garden and you can then vary these elements and introduce others in order to suit the needs of your own garden or your individual preferences.

Above: *The autumn colours of maple leaves are reflected in the pond at Tenju-an. Much of this garden dates back to the 13th century, with its simple design of two ponds, two islands and rocks arranged around a waterfall.*

Red pine

Cherry blossom

Japanese-style bridge

Pine island

Black pine

Clay-lined pond

Japanese maple

Grass

Waterfall

Above: *The most stable way to support the edges of a pond is to use rocks, even if you want grass to grow close to those edges.*

TYPICAL FEATURES

The following elements are the most important to include in a pond garden:

• ponds with rocks around the edges and cobble and sandy beaches shelving into the water;

• one or two islands, typically planted with pines and grasses among rocks;

• red-painted Chinese-style bridge;

• meandering stream or waterfall feeding the pond;

• boathouse with small boat;

• undulating hills around the pond;

• winding gravel paths;

• plants such as cherry trees, Japanese maples, kerria, azalea, spiraea.

PLANNING AND VISUALIZATION

First think about the site you are planning to use and how it might need to be adapted for a pond garden. A series of features such as these would have a minimum area requirement of 45 x 45m (147 x 147ft). The size, position and style of a pond will need to fit the location, and you may also want to imitate ponds you have seen in other gardens.

When you are choosing a site for a waterfall, find the most natural place in your garden for a fall, ideally a raised hill from which the waterfall flow can be created. If you want to build islands in the pond, these must be planned before you build the pond. Sketch your ideas for how the garden will look and what will be included. The coloured design opposite shows how an initial concept and visualization of this scene might work and how the elements will link together when everything is in place.

WATER PRACTICALITIES

Water sources It is obviously essential to have a source of water. If you own a natural source, such as a spring or a stream, make sure that it is sufficient to keep the pond clear and healthy in the dry summer months. If not, or if you have no natural source, consult a water garden specialist on what type and size of pump you will need for your pond. Remember that the power of the pump you need has a cost implication for running the electricity to drive the pump.

Loss of water You should also get advice on how to top up the pond from losses due to evaporation, and from inevitable leakages and splashing.

Draining excess water You will need to make provision for too much water from excessive rain, and also allow for drainage.

Making a pond with a soil liner

For creating a small pond the flexible liner method shown on pages 50–51 is the best option; this liner is easy to install and readily available at garden centres. Alternatively, a large-scale pond may be required, one to include in a pond or stroll garden with more generous dimensions. In this case you can use either a natural clay liner, or more conveniently an enhanced soil liner or geosynthetic clay liner, shown in the method below. Manmade liners such as these are now more commonly used than clay.

A natural clay liner needs to be created from naturally occurring clay within the garden site. It is also advisable to get professional advice for this type of pond because it has to integrate within the natural landscape of the site. Because of these requirements, if you want a substantial pond, especially one that won't be damaged by aquatic animals or other wildlife, an enhanced soil liner such as the one shown here is usually a safer choice, while having many of the advantages of a natural clay liner.

In the following method, a synthetic clay liner is combined with sodium bentonite crystals to produce a strong seal. For effective installation, the pond should be empty.

Sodium bentonite can be used either in the construction of a new pond, or to repair an existing pond. It is absorbed into the soil at the base of the pond and then swells to create a block so the moisture cannot escape. Treating a pond in this way will create a watertight seal

Above: *Synthetic clay liners are the best method of sealing large ponds in areas where there is no natural clay subsoil to use for the job.*

that will last for many years. What is more, it is environmentally friendly and safe to use. Make sure you use a high quality sodium bentonite, apply it following the manufacturer's instructions and use the recommended amount depending on your soil type and the area that is being treated.

You will need

- string, sand or canes for marking the outline of the pond
- 5 x 5cm (2 x 2in) stakes (for a pond more than 2m (6½ft) across)
- a laser level
- a spade
- rolls of synthetic clay liner that are sufficient to cover the sides and floor of the pond, allowing for a 15cm (6in) overlap between each sheet
- a sufficient quantity of sodium bentonite crystals to cover each of the overlapped joints of the liner to expand and seal it
- garden hose
- topsoil to overlap the liner by 30cm (12in)
- a tile or stone slab

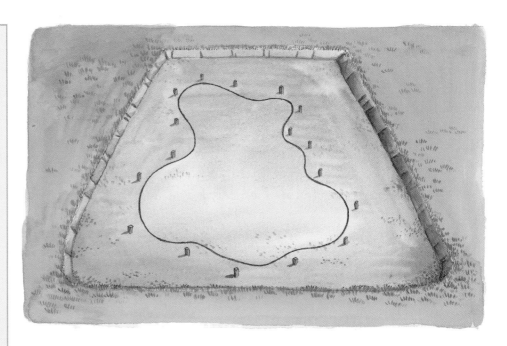

1 Remove at least 30cm (12in) of soil to a generous distance from the main working area and stockpile it for later use. If this excavation goes into the subsoil, keep the topsoil and subsoil in separate piles. Mark out the outline of the pond on the ground with string or sand or with a series of canes. With a large pond, drive in the stakes to indicate the level of water, as shown here.

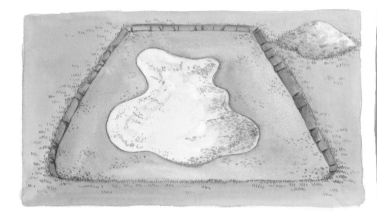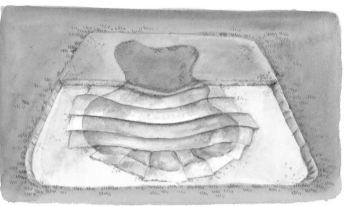

2 Excavate a saucer-shaped depression to a minimum of 60cm (2ft) and a maximum of 1.25m (4ft) at the deepest point. The sides should slope at no more than 30 degrees. Save the soil for replacing on the pond liner later and for grading around the sides.

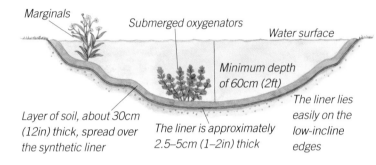

Marginals

Submerged oxygenators

Water surface

Minimum depth of 60cm (2ft)

Layer of soil, about 30cm (12in) thick, spread over the synthetic liner

The liner is approximately 2.5–5cm (1–2in) thick

The liner lies easily on the low-incline edges

Above: *A cross-section of a synthetic clay-lined pond.*

Below: *A large and complex pond like that at Syoki-ho-en could be lined using clay or a geosynthetic clay liner.*

3 Roll sheets of the liner over the excavation and over the edges of the pond, overlapping them by about 15cm (6in). Sprinkle sodium bentonite crystals between and over the joints: once they absorb water, they will swell to fill any cracks, so completing the seal.

4 Cover the liner with a 30cm (12in) layer of soil, avoiding soil with heavy levels of fertilizer. The liner expands when in contact with water to several times its original thickness. This process will reverse and the mat may crack if it is allowed to dry out, so once the mat is in contact with moisture, either from rain or from the soil layer, keep it wet by laying a plastic sheet over the completed areas or by sprinkling it until you are ready to fill the pond.

5 Add water by resting the end of a garden hose on a tile or stone slab and letting the water in slowly. This prevents the freshly added soil from being dislodged.

6 Fine particles of debris, silt and clay suspended in the water may take several days or weeks to settle on the bottom, but the water will then begin to clear.

Making a pine island

A pine island can be one of the finest features of a traditional Japanese pond garden. This small rocky island would be planted with a twisted, weatherbeaten pine tree, and is reminiscent of the Matsushima islands off northern Japan (*matsu* means "pine" in Japanese). A pond of virtually any size could accommodate a small pine island, though obviously the pond and island will need to be in suitable proportions to achieve the desired effect. These islands are best surrounded by stones, which give a more natural look to the feature and can also be used to support the soil.

Although it is possible to build an island after the pond has been made, it is always advisable to plan for an island during the pond-building process, rather than as an afterthought. Driving machinery or wheelbarrows across butyl-lined or clay-lined pools could damage the lining. If, however, the pond has been made, make a layer at least 30cm (12in) deep of protective soil, free of sharp stones, over a clay liner, or simply roll back a butyl liner.

Japanese black pines (*Pinus thunbergii*) are the best variety for pine islands as they can be easily shaped to give a picturesque windswept habit and they are also tolerant of wet roots. They do not like waterlogged soils, so build up

Above: *This pine island is located in the tranquil lake setting of the 19th-century Heian shrine, in Kyoto.*

the island to at least 60cm (2ft) higher than the water level to ensure that the pine roots have plenty of soil, not only to grow in but also to ensure they are sturdy enough to withstand winds.

PINE ISLAND PRACTICALITIES

Size The size of the island should be in proportion to the size of pond.

Shape Small islands should be simple in shape. Larger islands can have a more interesting outline.

Bridges If the island is close enough to the edge of the pond, you can link it to the mainland with a bridge.

Foundations Make sure that the foundations are at least twice the area of the exposed island.

Plants Pines do not like waterlogged roots, so make sure they have access to dry soil. Dwarf miscanthus looks good with pines and rocks.

Wild areas Leave some long grass to encourage wildfowl to nest.

Rocks Rocks blend well with pine trees. You can make a turtle or crane island by suggesting the shape with rocks.

You will need
- underlay and flexible liner
- scissors to cut underlay
- a number of rocks to support the soil
- interestingly shaped rocks to place on the pine island
- topsoil
- a spade
- a crowbar
- a wheelbarrow or small dumper truck
- a Japanese black pine tree (more than one in different sizes will also look good)
- grass seed or any ornamental grasses to decorate the island, including *Miscanthus yakushimenis* and *Molinia caerulea*

CONSTRUCTING A PINE ISLAND OVER A BUTYL LINER

1 Drain the pond, if necessary, then roll back the butyl liner and underlay. Make a large mound of soil where you want your island to be.

2 Lay the underlay and flexible liner over the top of the soil mound. Cut a hole in the underlay and liner so that an area of soil is exposed, but ensure that the liner is taken well above the waterline.

3 Add a further mound of soil on top of the foundation to create a gently curving island. Stack rocks on top of each other all around the edge of the island in order to hold the dry soil in place.

4 Plant the pine(s) and sow the grass seed, or plant grass plants. Keep well watered until established.

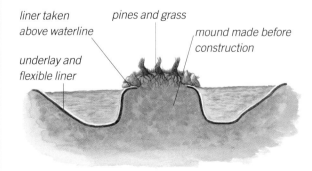

liner taken above waterline *pines and grass* *mound made before construction* *underlay and flexible liner*

Above: *This method ensures that the pine roots do not become waterlogged.*

CONSTRUCTING A PINE ISLAND OVER A CLAY OR SYNTHETIC CLAY LINER

1 Drain the pond, if necessary, then protect the clay liner with an extra 30cm (12in) of soil. If draining is not possible, use a tracked vehicle to build the island. Alternatively, you could use a large digger with a long reach, if the island is made close enough to the edge of the pond.

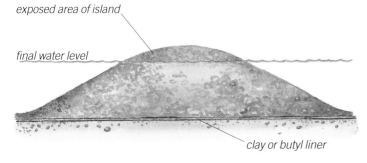

exposed area of island

final water level

clay or butyl liner

2 Build a mound of soil that will be the base of the island over the top of the liner. There is no need to roll the matting over the island. Make sure that the sides slope at no more than 30 degrees, which will keep the banks stable.

3 Keep building the island up with soil until it is 60–100cm (24–40in) above the water line. This will give the pine tree plenty of water-free root room in which to grow. There is no need to shape the mound at this stage.

Below: *A good example of a well-shaped Japanese black pine on a rocky islet. The island is suggestive of a turtle, with the upright stones to the right of the island representing its head.*

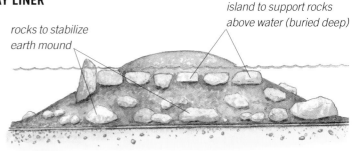

ring of rocks set around island to support rocks above water (buried deep)

rocks to stabilize earth mound

4 Bury rocks deeply all over the mound, from the base up to just below the water line. These will be the foundation for any rocks above water.

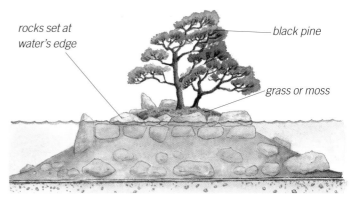

rocks set at water's edge

black pine

grass or moss

5 Build up an arrangement of rocks on top to imitate a rocky island. Shape the mound to look naturalistic. Add more soil between some of the rocks and use one of these crevices to plant a pine tree. Scatter grass seed over the soil areas in the autumn or spring and water well. Plant some ornamental grasses between one or two of the rocks.

Building a waterfall

Waterfalls were an important feature of Heian pond gardens. They were regarded as the abode of Fudo, an important personification of the Buddha, while the two main supporting stones were considered to be the Buddha's attendants. As a plentiful, natural, life-giving source, water was regarded as sacred, and waterfalls therefore tended to be well camouflaged in the landscape. The *Sakuteiki* says "There are many ways to make a waterfall, but no matter what, they should always face the moon, so that falling water will reflect in the moonlight."

First choose the "waterfall stone", the one that the water actually spills over. This will determine the height of the fall. You may decide to build a series of falls, but remember that a large amount of water does not necessarily mean a better effect. A small waterfall falling from a height of 1m (40in) into shallow water or on to a carp stone, a tumbling cascade or a plain sheet of water can be just as effective. Always follow the "desire" of the stones and the way they want to direct the water. If you are using a recycling system with an electric pump, try to minimize the amount of water that will be lost through splashing.

Above: *The sound of a trickling waterfall can create as much atmosphere as a torrent. A stone is often placed at the bottom, at the point at which the water falls, to make a feature of the sound. A notable example of this is the stone at the Dragon Gate cascade in Kinkaku-ji.*

WATERFALL PRACTICALITIES

Spillage Use a butyl liner to contain any potential water spillage.

Sound When planning, think of the sound effects as well as appearance.

Security Bed the base stones well into concrete to make a secure beginning.

Flow Test the water flow as you place stones using a hose to see the effect.

Control Be patient and flexible, water is difficult to manage when it is in freefall.

Flow rate The waterfall will change character if the flow rate is changed. If you are using a pump, make sure you buy one with a variable flow valve so you can manage the water flow to suit your waterfall.

You will need
- a good selection of large rocks to suit the shape of the proposed waterfall
- a spade
- a crowbar
- a large sheet of butyl rubber to fit the dimensions of the waterfall (note that you need to lay wider than the fall itself)
- a strip of liner sealing tape (optional if pond is clay lined)
- concreting sand and cement
- a wheelbarrow
- a concrete mixer (optional)
- machinery, such as a sack truck or skid loader for moving rocks if they are too heavy and awkward to move by hand
- perhaps a good friend to help

HOW TO CONSTRUCT A WATERFALL

1 First make an outline sketch of how you would like the waterfall to look. Then mark out the proposed position on the ground. If you have already made a selection of rocks, these will help to decide the design; otherwise, select special rocks to suit the intended shape of your cascade.

2 Dig out an area three or four times wider than the waterfall itself. This will give you plenty of room to work and to spread out a large sheet of butyl liner. The liner will lie under the whole structure of the waterfall so that any splashes and leakages will find their way back into the pond.

The liner is laid wider than the waterfall

Stones to weight down liner

The waterfall liner overlaps the pond liner, creating a sealed joint

3 If the pond has a butyl liner, lift up the edge of the liner and tuck it under the waterfall liner. The pond liner should be well above the pond water level. Seal the two liners together with the sealing strip. If the pond is clay lined, let the waterfall liner drop under the waterline.

4 Make a firm concrete base for the first foundation stones. These may be the two main supporting stones or simply the base from which you can build up a series of stones for a cascade-style waterfall.

5 Measure where you expect the water to fall and erect the main stone. Seal the joints between it and the main supporting stones.

6 You will need to build a header pool, even if the waterfall is being fed by a stream. The header pool will help to keep the flow of water constant.

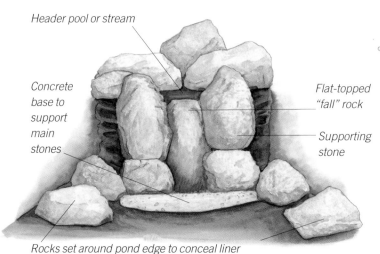

Header pool or stream

Concrete base to support main stones

Flat-topped "fall" rock

Supporting stone

Rocks set around pond edge to conceal liner

7 Add more rocks to the sides and above the header pool to make a naturalistic setting and to help retain the soil on the steep sides. Make provision for some soil pockets to plant sedges, ferns and other waterside plants. Make sure all concrete joints are skilfully disguised.

Below: *With a natural water course and interesting contours, you can recreate the effects of a mountain stream. The Tully Japanese Garden has carefully observed the rocks and flow of natural streams.*

Cobbles and shingle at base of waterfall in shallow water

Fern

Concealed edge of liner

Hosta

Carp stone

8 Allow the waterfall base to open up by positioning a number of smaller stones and cobbles there. Having observed the flow of the water, place a "carp stone" at the base to receive the water, which will spill over and around it.

BUILDING A STREAM AND WATERFALL SYSTEM

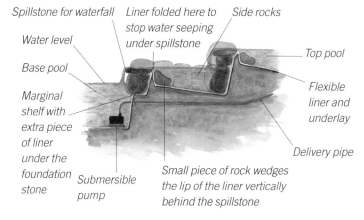

Spillstone for waterfall

Liner folded here to stop water seeping under spillstone

Side rocks

Water level

Top pool

Base pool

Flexible liner and underlay

Marginal shelf with extra piece of liner under the foundation stone

Submersible pump

Small piece of rock wedges the lip of the liner vertically behind the spillstone

Delivery pipe

DRY GARDENS

Dry gardens are often referred to as *kare-sansui*, which literally means "dry mountain water". This is a style of garden in which water has been replaced by sand, gravel or pebbles. These gardens have also become synonymous with what we now often call a Zen garden. Dry gardens were conceived by the Japanese with abstract designs, often just consisting of gravel, and as deeply spiritual and symbolic landscapes. They can also be enjoyed by visitors as peaceful and restorative environments where they can be appreciated for their calm beauty.

Dry gardens have inspired garden designers throughout the world and through history. An understanding or, better still, an experience of Zen will help you to find their spiritual essence, but another way to look at dry gardens is to see them as minimalist landscape art.

When you first plan a dry garden, try to imagine a distant misty mountain landscape, a stream with waterfalls or a rocky shoreline. Look at how streams and rivers flow, how waves lap against rocks, and you will learn how to use the inspiration of nature in your own garden, to make raked gravel patterns around specially and significantly arranged rocks.

Above: *The Mystic Isles rock arrangement in the dry garden at Tofuku-ji is thought to have immense power.*
Left: *The symmetrical layout contrasts with the natural forms of Japanese maples in the dry garden at Tenju-an, Kyoto.*

The dry garden style

The dry garden is the most contemplative of all the Japanese garden styles. It is also the most abstract. You do need a fairly good understanding of the origins of this style to make one that is truly effective. Have a look at photos of the famous dry Zen gardens of Japan, and see if you think that your site would be suitable. You will also need to keep it tidy, so it's not an ideal choice for a large family garden. Dry gardens are especially well suited to courtyards and small enclosed spaces – even those areas that are inhospitable to plants.

Above: *Dry gardens use gravel and rocks to suggest the flow and expanse of water in its different forms.*

ELEMENTS OF A DRY GARDEN

As its name suggests, a dry garden's essential elements are dry materials in the form of sand and gravel, which are often raked into patterns, and carefully chosen and strategically placed rocks. Another important element is a flat site, as the extensive use of sand and gravel means that a level surface is highly preferable to a slope.

Sand and gravel

The "dry" aspect of the garden consists of sand or gravel spread to represent an expanse of water, either in the form of the sea or a lake. Dry gardens might also contain a dry "stream" and a dry "waterfall", although these are not essential. The use of all this dry material means that dry gardens need very little maintenance: the occasional raking of the gravel (and the trimming of any shrubs that might be included) is all that is required.

The sand and gravel will usually be contained within a rectangular frame. (In Japan, they are found in rectangular courtyards in Zen temples.)

Rocks

Once you have established that your garden is suitable, the key to a successful dry garden is in the arrangements of the rocks. There are many arrangements to choose from, for example a Buddhist grouping, where a central stone represents the Buddha or the sacred mountain Mount Shumisen; a grouping that represents different aspects of the Mystic Isles of immortals; or an arrangement simply placed with intuition and instinct – you will have to try this one out by moving your rocks until you are happy with the effect. All of these arrangements should be designed with a sense of the tranquil, and should avoid any excessive forms in shape or size.

Plants

If rocks are difficult to obtain, or you have decided not to use them, interesting arrangements can also be made with groups of plants clipped to the shape of distant hills or to represent sacred sites.

Left: *Mirei Shigemori, in his finest work at Tofuku-ji, used bold groups of rocks and stylized gravel raking, to illustrate the ancient Chinese myth of the Mystic Isles.*

Left: *Most dry gardens are designed in courtyards, where the rectangular shape in a sense represents the frame of a painting, while the spread of sand represents the white "unpainted" canvas. Despite this, they can be equally effective and suggestive in more naturalistic surroundings, such as this example in Kew Gardens in England, although it is more difficult to play with the sense of scale.*

Below: *Rocks set near the edge of an expanse of gravel can suggest a river or lakeside. Well-placed rocks need simple plantings to enhance their form: these rocks at Kew are set against a plain wall with a dramatically pruned pine.*

How to make a dry garden

Dry gardens are generally best sited on level ground, unless you intend to include a dry waterfall, but even this can be built up in one corner of the garden. A garden called the Daisen-in in the Daitokuji Temple in Kyoto portrays an entire mountain landscape and has almost all the elements of a dry garden: rocks and bent pines, dry streams, a dry waterfall, a natural stone slab bridge and even a block of stone "floating" on the sea of sand. Here is a suggestion for a dry garden design that incorporates these key features, all contained in a defined rectangular area. The planting is restricted to a pine and some bamboo, interspersed with stones and rocks and surrounded by raked gravel. The three stages of creating this garden are shown in the following pages: positioning rocks, placing edging stones and improving drainage.

Above: *While dry gardens are popularly known as Zen gardens, the Japanese name is* kare-sansui, *which translates as "dry mountain water", with sand or gravel representing water and the rocks the mountains.*

pruned pine

bamboo

tiled wall capping

painted plaster wall

rock set in line of stone edging

cobbles

raked gravel (concentric ripple pattern)

main rock arrangement

raked gravel (parallel lines or stream current)

stone edging

TYPICAL FEATURES OF A DRY GARDEN

A dry garden should be a rectangular level courtyard within three walls, the fourth side used as a viewing platform and including the following:

• a rectangle of edging stones or tiles to frame the garden;

• rocks of interesting shapes;

• gravel, preferably a light silvery grey;

• moss around the bases of rocks to make them look like islands;

• stepping stones and lanterns ;

• bent pines and small-leaved evergreens to tuck around the rocks;

• clipped azaleas to imitate hills;

• dry waterfalls and landscapes with dry streams and bridges.

PLANNING AND VISUALIZATION

Before you start you must have a good idea of the elements you want to introduce and be certain that you can get all of them to the site. Rocks are especially difficult to move in narrow confines, but mini-diggers can get through openings of around 1m (1yd) wide, which might be sufficient. If you are contemplating growing plants in your dry garden, make sure the soil is right for them. If there is no soil on site or the drainage is poor, you can build up planting areas between rock arrangements or dig trenches to improve the drainage.

ROCKS, EDGING AND GRAVEL

The first priority is to get the rocks in place as this will be the most awkward and messy job. After this, you can frame your "picture" with edging stones that will contain the area of gravel and will set off both the gravel

Above: *This dry garden was made on the site of an old barn with little or no soil. This factor, combined with the old walls and level site, made a dry garden the natural choice.*

and the rocks. In Japan these edges are often quite elaborate, using a combination of tiles, strips of granite, and a row of cobbles that doubles up as a drainage channel. Even if you are using a more contemporary design, unconfined in an open space, it will still be necessary to build an edge to contain the gravel or sand.

The gravel will need to be spread around 5–6cm (2–2½in) deep if you intend to rake it into patterns. It can be less deep if you want the gravel to be a practical element that can be walked over. However, the spiritual, Zen quality of a dry garden is more effectively achieved by the creation of elements for both viewing and contemplation.

Positioning rocks

Rocks are seen as important natural symbols of strength. They are used in many Japanese gardens, with the order and positioning seen as key to the balance of the garden. They can vary from monumental sizes that need digging in and cementing to stabilize them, to smaller rocks that can be moved by hand. Rocks should always be placed in a naturalistic manner, so that they look balanced in relation to each other. Traditional Japanese gardeners, attributing a living spirit to rocks, described this as "following their desire".

Above: *Rocks with interesting grain patterns and markings are ideal for dry gardens.*

The placing of rocks is a crucial aspect of Japanese gardening. You may choose to employ professional landscapers, but with some guidance it is possible to organize it yourself, so that you understand the process, from hiring the right equipment to all the safety issues. Once you have established how you are going to move them, you will need to know how to position them both safely and artistically. Establish the rough weight of the rocks so that you can be advised on the right size of machinery and correct gauge of lifting straps.

You will need

- two people to carry the rock
- protective clothing (e.g. hard hat, gloves and boots)
- strong straps (from a hire shop)
- a scaffolding pole and shackle
- a spade and a crowbar
- smaller propping stones
- a fencing stake
- a sledgehammer
- loose soil for backfilling

ROCK PRACTICALITIES

Finding rocks It may be hard to find rocks that match your artistic intentions exactly, so be flexible when arranging them.

Buying rocks Allow yourself one or two extra ones to give more choice.

Placing rocks Move back from time to time to a different vantage point. The rocks must look right from all possible viewing angles.

Adjusting rocks Take your time to make sure the rocks feel right. It may seem like hard work, but large rocks will be very difficult to move later, once the garden is established.

Leaving rocks Once you have set the rocks and finished the garden, it will be virtually impossible to move any of the bigger rocks without considerable disruption.

1 Decide which way round and up you want the rock to be. Then measure the amount of rock that will show above ground and how much needs to be buried. Tall upright rocks will need to be buried deep to ensure they are stable. The more angled you want the rock to be, the deeper the hole should be.

2 Draw a line with a piece of chalk to indicate ground level on the rock. Measure again so that you know how deep to dig the receiving hole, taking into account the extra 4–6cm (1½–2½in) of gravel that will be laid over the area.

3 Dig the hole, and lay a fencing stake, with a spirit level on it, across the top, raised to the height of the finished gravel.

4 Check the hole has been dug to the right depth. Digging too deep may make the soil loose below the rock and cause it to "settle" too much. Allow for plenty of room each side for packing and adjusting the angle of the rock.

5 Using a digger, lower the strapped-up rock very slowly into the hole. Two people should be in place to help to guide the rock as it is lowered, twisting it so that it is angled correctly.

6 With the rock safely strapped up and attached to the lifting gear, try out different angles and positions until you are satisfied that it is placed where you want it.

7 Keeping the rock still strapped up and attached to the digger, support the undersides and sides of the rock with smaller stones. These can also be used to wedge between two rocks for support.

8 Use a sledgehammer to ram the stones tightly into place. Then test the rock for its overall stability. The rock should be in a "rock solid" position even before you start to pack around it with soil.

9 Backfill the hole with a loamy or clay soil. Sandy soil will not pack well and is far too loose. With the butt end of a fencing stake, ram the soil between the stones.

10 Ram the final layers of soil firmly around the rock with a sledgehammer.

11 Rake the surrounding soil until it is level. Set the accompanying rocks in place. In this case they are smaller and lower, and therefore don't need such a deep and solid foundation.

12 The final stage of the process is to water the soil in around the rocks to remove all air pockets and to help compact the ground.

MOVING ROCKS

There are various practical considerations to bear in mind when positioning rocks:

• move large rocks with a hired mini-digger

• use tough nylon/canvas fibre straps to minimize damage to the rock;

• so you can calculate the foundation depth, decide which part of the rock will be visible in the finished garden;

• dig the hole slightly deeper than you

need so you have the flexibility to adjust the position later;

• try the rock in different positions and angles before removing the straps;

• check the rock for stability and fill in tightly with soil.

Placing edging stones

Most dry gardens are set within a framed space, whether it be in the open with a fenced area or in a courtyard with existing walls surrounding the space. This framing serves both to contain the dry sand or gravel and to make the garden look more like a painting hung within a frame. In all the famous dry gardens, you will notice the considerable care that is taken in choosing the edging materials and how they are laid. Long pavers of granite or dark blue tiles, or both, can be used with a channel of cobbles between them as an aid to drainage.

In your own garden, you can use any native materials. For this project lengths of stone made of the same local sandstone as the rocks have been used. These edging stones are fairly uniform but by no means perfect rectangles. These stones are being used to separate a border of cobbles against the surrounding wall from the dry sea of gravel.

Above: *Edging stones not only help to separate planting areas from gravelled areas but can also make decorative features of their own, such as this raised area in the Tully Japanese Garden. The Japanese pay close attention to detail in all parts of the garden.*

You will need
- a hand-picked selection of stones
- builder's twine and pegs
- a tape measure
- a spirit level
- a pick
- concreting sand and cement
- a shovel
- a rubber-headed hammer
- a brick-laying trowel
- weed-suppressing fabric
- scissors
- cobbles
- a rock to break up the uniformity of the edging (optional)

EDGING MATERIALS

The following materials can be used for framing areas of the dry garden:

- local or salvaged materials;
- old, slightly misshapen bricks;
- old granite setts;
- old roofing or floor tiles set on edge;
- charred wooden post tops.

1 Set up a builder's line parallel to one of the walls and mark the level of the outside of the edging stones, using a tape measure to check that it is an equal distance from the wall at both ends. On a flat site, use a spirit level to check the line is level. On a sloping site, set the line up tightly at either end of the edging run. Dig out a trench for the edging stones, a little deeper and wider than the stones themselves, always keeping an eye on the line. Lay out your row of edging stones so that they are easily reached.

2 Make a concreting mix using soft or sharp sand mix, eight parts sand to one part cement (most cement will have mixture recommendations on the bags). Small amounts of concrete can be easily mixed in a wheelbarrow with a spade but larger amounts might require a concrete mixer. Towable concrete mixers, both electrical and petrol-powered, can be hired from plant hire depots. Shovel a small amount into the trench, enough to set 1m (1yd) of edging stones at a time.

3 Set one of the edging stones on to the cement bed so that it sits slightly higher than the builder's line.

4 Using the hammer, tap the stone firmly until it becomes level with the line. Repeat with the other stones until the path edge is complete. The stone ends should be close enough to prevent sand and gravel slipping between them.

5 Shore up the edging stones with the concreting mix, making sure that the mix will not show above the finished gravel.

6 Spread some soft sand between the edging stones and the wall. Remove any stones or blocks of earth that are still protruding.

7 Measure, cut and lay weed-suppressing fabric over the layer of soft sand and tuck in the edges well.

8 Spread a layer of cobbles over the fabric, keeping the level of the cobbles below the top of the stones.

9 For an unusual touch, place a natural rock, one that can be easily moved using a sack truck, into a pre-measured gap. Scoop out 6–10cm (2½–4in) of soil and spread a layer of 4cm (1½in) of sharp sand, then lay the rock directly on to the bed of sharp sand.

Improving drainage

Drainage requirements must be carefully considered in the early stages of planning a dry garden, especially if you are intending to grow plants. Dry gardens are most frequently created on level sites, and often close to buildings, where heavy machinery and ground works may have caused compaction of the natural texture of the soil. This is especially true of gardens built on clay soils or on a concrete base. In such situations, flexible drainage pipes may need to be laid to improve the drainage.

Poor drainage will kill plants and may cause damage to buildings and walls. If a dry garden is constructed over badly drained heavy clay soil, the water will stay on the surface after heavy rain once the rocks and edging stones are in place. To remedy this, the best solution is to lay a network of feeder drains and a main drain to ensure that the water can flow away naturally.

Above: *On some level sites you will need to make allowance for drainage. This can be set around the edge of the dry garden and made into a design detail of its own. A trench filled with large gravel or cobbles may be enough to disguise such areas.*

You will need
- 10cm- (4in-) diameter flexible perforated drainage pipe
- angled joints
- a sharp knife
- a spade and shovel
- a wheelbarrow
- a hose
- 10–20mm (½–¾in) pea gravel
- crushed stone with stone dust (known as scalpings or hoggin)
- coloured gravel or sand
- a roller or wacker-plate
- a rake

1 Mark the layout of the drains with marker paint. Then dig the main drain to a depth of at least 45cm (18in) and the feeder drains, closer to the surface, at 30–35cm (12–14in) deep. The trenches should slope to give a fall of at least 10cm (4in) per 20m (20yd).

2 Spread a layer of pea gravel (small, smooth, rounded stones) 4cm (1½in) deep in the bottom of the trench.

3 Lay the flexible drainage pipe in the trench and check that the slope allows an effective fall of water by filling with a hose at the top end. Cover the pipe with at least a further 10cm (4in) of gravel. Leave uncovered in places where the feeder pipes will join it.

4 Cut the main pipe at the places where the feeder pipes (from the planted areas) will join it. (The perforated drainage pipes can easily be cut with a sharp knife.)

5 At the junctions of the feeder drains to the main drain, you will need to fit angled joints. These joints are often designed to take different sized pipes; cut out the size that fits your chosen pipe sizes. Once again, cover over all the pipes with gravel.

6 Spread a 5–7.5cm (2–3in) layer of crushed stone/stone dust mix over the entire area of the dry garden where the raked sand or gravel will eventually be.

7 Spread the layer until it is level, filling in potholes and making sure the drainage trenches are filled in. The roller will not be able to firm in narrow trenches so these should be compressed with your feet. This will help to avoid any subsidence later on.

DRAINAGE PRACTICALITIES

Soak-away You will need to check for the nearest point for collecting storm water. If this is at some distance, you should construct a soak-away or French drain to collect the drain water.

Location Check the location for all services, such as sewerage pipes, electric cables, gas pipes and mains water pipes, before you dig any trenches and before you decide where to lay the main drain.

Flow Check how the drainage levels will work. The principle to follow is that the main drain must be dug to the lowest level, so that all the drains on the site can feed into it. This can be done by eye and by feeding a hose into one of the drains to check for flow, or by using levelling equipment for more precise measurements.

Fall The fall for a drain should be no less than 10cm (4in) in every 20m (20yd).

Capacity On large sites, a larger main drain of 15cm (6in) diameter may be required.

8 Using the mechanical wacker-plate or a roller, compact the surface. If any subsidence occurs in this process, fill in any depressions with more crushed stone and roll again, until the whole surface is perfectly level.

9 Spread the gravel or sand over the surface to the required depth and rake it level. For sand that will be raked in patterns the depth should be at least 6cm (2½in).

Right: *On this site, the subsoil was of solid clay so a drainage pipe was laid around the perimeter of the garden. Additional drains feed from the planting holes into the main drain.*

TEA GARDENS

Tea gardens were designed as places in which to appreciate *sado*, the tea-drinking ceremony. These spaces were seen to represent a break in a journey from a busy urban centre to a secluded country retreat. The design and philosophy of the tea garden can easily be adapted for the modern garden, and suits city life now as much as it did in the 16th century. Once the significance of the tea garden has been grasped, you can be as creative as you want, just like designers throughout history.

All you really need for a tea garden is a path – the whole point of a tea garden is to be able to create an illusion of wandering through a wild mountainside – but you can also include a range of typical decorative features, such as gates, water basins and lanterns. The onus is placed on the guests to comprehend that the journey they are taking is "real", but to help them, the garden designer will include pointers and hints as to the symbolic nature of each element.

The basic principles of the tea garden should be adapted to suit the aspirations and taste of the owner. While one tea master might enjoy a natural look, another might prefer a creative mix of the manmade and the natural.

Above: *A special lacquered table is prepared for an outdoor tea ceremony (no-ta-de), often conducted in an informal style.*
Left: *Most tea gardens have a* tsukubai *arrangement – a low water basin filled with fresh water and accompanied by a lantern.*

The tea garden style

This type of garden is characterized by pathways and thresholds, and represents a journey to a more spiritual world. You enter a tea garden through a covered outer gateway, or *sotomon*. Inside, the garden is divided into two halves: an outer area, where a small waiting room can be placed, and an inner area, where the tea house will be found. Linking the two areas is the path, or *roji*, which leads the visitor past shelter seats and through a stooping gate to reach the ultimate goal: the tea house itself and the host within who waits to welcome the guests.

Above: *Water basins and lanterns were originally set alongside the tea paths of Japanese gardens as part of the tea ceremony.*

ELEMENTS OF A TEA GARDEN

There are four important elements that make up a Japanese tea garden: the tea house, the path or *roji* (dewy path) and garden around it, lanterns to line the path, and a water basin.

Tea house

A tea house is traditionally a rustic building set within a tea garden. It can be quite small and hidden away in a secluded place, but in later Japanese gardens it became a more open building placed with a view over the garden. This makes it more like a tea arbour, or a gazebo. The original essence of the tea house was as a "mountain place in the city", a secluded rustic hermitage and retreat from busy lives.

Path

The path, usually a stepping-stone path, will pass by the waiting room and through a small "stooping gate" – encouraging visitors to be aware of the world they are leaving behind and the wilderness and realms of higher

Left: *Reaching the tea house is the ultimate goal of a tea garden. The route typically consists of gateways that mark significant stages of the journey, and the tea house itself can often not be viewed until the final stage.*

consciousness ahead. The wilderness does not need to be literal – it can be suggested by "mountain" plants, usually glossy-leaved evergreens such as camellias and aucubas, planted under a canopy of maples.

Lanterns and water basins
The path and the area around the main water basin should be lit by carefully positioned lanterns, originally because tea ceremonies were often held in the evening. The water basin is an important feature representing the need for cleansing before entering the tea house.

Right: *The veranda pillars at Hosen-in frame the scene from the tea house.*

Below: *Shelter seats are placed alongside the tea path for guests to wait in comfort before they are summoned to the tea house.*

How to make a tea garden

The art of creating a Japanese tea garden is not just in placing the features: it requires some understanding of the philosophy behind the tea ceremony. Once familiar with this, you can combine the elements of the stepping-stone path, lanterns, water basins and plants into a style that is both unified and unique to your own tastes and culture. The tea garden adapts well to small areas: the essential wandering path can be as short as 5m (around 16ft), though in a large garden it could be 30m (100ft) or more. The practical sequences that follow you will show you how to create the main features of a tea garden: arranging a *tsukubai*, setting a lantern and laying a stepping-stone path. The example shown below combines all the elements; there is room for a tea house, but the path will lead to a "tea room" in the house itself.

Above: *A tall water basin of this type would commonly be found next to a veranda in a courtyard garden, or as a self-contained unit on the "spiritual" journey to the tea house through the tea garden.*

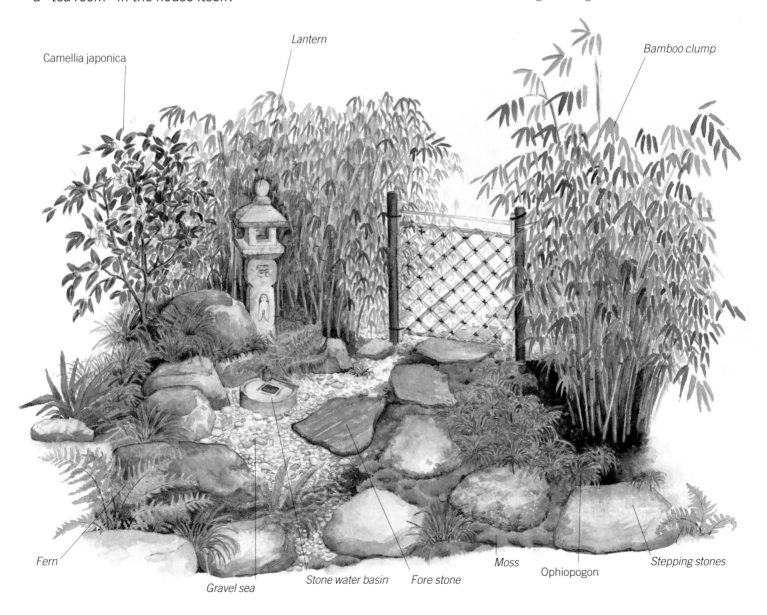

Camellia japonica

Lantern

Bamboo clump

Fern

Gravel sea

Stone water basin

Fore stone

Moss

Ophiopogon

Stepping stones

PLANNING AND VISUALIZATION

Once you have established the goal of the tea path (i.e. the tea house or tea room), you will want to work out an intriguing journey for the path to take. At some point on the path, look for a suitable place to create the *tsukubai* arrangement – the combination of the water basin and lantern. If your tea garden is large, you might want to divide the garden into two halves – an inner and outer *roji* – placing a waiting room in the inner garden and a middle crawl-through gate to divide them. Build up the planting to suggest a wilderness, with rocks informally placed at the sides of the path, using ferns and sedges and also including other plants tucked in among them.

Even if you have only a very small space, try to place all the elements to create the sense of a journey that leaves the busy world behind, so that you and your guests can feel you are entering a place of spiritual purity.

TYPICAL FEATURES OF A TEA GARDEN

In addition to the tea house or tea room, the following are usual elements:

• an entrance gate;

• a winding stepping-stone path;

• a water basin with cobbles around it;

• lanterns to light the path and basin;

• a waiting room or bench for guests;

• a middle crawl-through gate;

• woodland planting of camellias, maples and bamboos, and low planting of ferns and sedges around rocks.

WATER BASIN

The simplest system is to source an attractive basin and fill the basin by hand, as you would a bird bath. But if you want your water basin to be constantly topped up, you will need to build a reservoir under the basin to receive the spillage. The water can then be drained to a soak-away, a pond or a mains drain, or be recycled by a small pump placed in the base of the reservoir. If you use an electric pump, and if you want an electric lantern, you will need an outdoor source of electricity that is both safe and fully weatherproofed.

Arranging a *tsukubai*

The *tsukubai* is one of the key ingredients of the tea garden. The term *tsukubai* means a low crouching basin that guests use to wash their hands and face, a spiritual cleansing before they enter the teahouse. It has also come to refer to the whole arrangement of the low water basin and its accompanying lantern, the paving stone that the guests stand on when they use the water basin, and the sea of gravel and cobbles around it. The paving stone, or laver stone, on which visitors stand, results in the lowering of the body before water, indicating humility.

The water basin is replenished with fresh water each time the tea guests arrive. This can be done either by manually emptying the basin and refilling it with a jug (pitcher) – the easiest method – or by a having a constantly dripping flow of water fed from a tap or natural spring via a bamboo pipe, which then overflows into the reservoir below, where the water is either drained away or recycled by an electric pump.

Above: *Water can be fed to the basin through a bamboo pipe. Allowing a tap to drip slowly but steadily at the source will ensure that you keep a constant supply of fresh water in the basin. Cleanliness and purity are viewed as sacred, and are crucial aspects of the Japanese tea ceremony.*

SETTING UP A *TSUKUBAI*

The elements that accompany the *tsukubai* are as important as the water basin itself for an authentic setting.

Rocks Place two or more flat-topped rocks on either side of the *tsukubai*. These are useful to stand a lantern on and for guests to place their personal effects on while they are washing themselves.

Cobbles Arrange a sea of cobbles around the *tsukubai*. While not essential, this makes an attractive surrounding for the basin as well as helping to keep the surface area around it dry.

Ladle Keep a bamboo ladle near or laid over the basin for guests to scoop up water to wash with. The ladle will need to be kept clean, as bamboo becomes mouldy quickly when it is left damp; alternatively you can place it by the basin only when guests are expected.

Drainage Provide a drainage outlet for larger basins (see pages 112–113).

You will need
- a spade
- a wheelbarrow
- a reservoir kit
- a water basin
- rocks
- a flat stepping stone
- large-diameter gravel or cobbles
- a bamboo spout (optional)

1 Having selected the position of your *tsukubai*, first dig a hole with a spade to accommodate the reservoir you have chosen. The hole should be made deep enough in order to leave the rim of the reservoir approximately 4cm (1½in) proud of the soil level.

2 Place the reservoir in the hole, check that it is level, backfill with sand and then firm it in place.

3 Level the surrounding soil for the area that will represent the "sea". If you are not recycling water from the reservoir (see pages 112–113) you could use a large plastic pot that can be filled with gravel to help with drainage. If you do this you will need to make sure there are adequate holes in the base of the pot for the water to drain through.

4 Spread a layer of sharp sand 4cm (1½in) deep over the soil area, so that it lies level with the rim of the reservoir. The sand will help both to keep the site clean and to act as a free-draining medium on to which to lay the cobbles. Place the metal grill over the reservoir and then lay a piece of fine plastic mesh over that. The mesh should be fine enough to prevent debris, soil or sand falling into the reservoir; this is especially critical if you intend to use a recycling pump, which can easily become blocked by debris.

5 Place a few cobbles to secure the mesh in place and lower the water basin on to the middle of the grill.

6 Spread a layer of cobbles or large gravel over the area to a depth where there is no soil, sand or mesh visible.

7 Collect the cobbles around the basin. Place your stepping stone next to the basin and firm it in so it is surrounded by cobbles or gravel.

8 Place the surface layer of cobbles by hand, arranging them so that they fit snugly together and lie in an attractive but natural manner.

Right: *Plant some ferns, sedge or ophiopogon close to the basin as well as around the surrounding rocks.*

Setting a lantern

Lanterns are integral to any Japanese tea garden. Originally they were found only outside Buddhist temples, but they were later introduced to the tea garden as the tea ceremony became influenced by Zen Buddhist symbolism. The lamps were lit as an offering to the Buddha, and early ones accommodated an oil lamp. Lanterns were also needed to light the tea path, as tea ceremonies often took place in the early evening. The stone lantern is an important connecting factor in the Japanese garden, as both a raw material and a manmade element.

Above: *Although most lanterns are placed as sculptural features in the tea garden, they are sometimes lit. This light is often very subdued.*

Once you have placed the *tsukubai*, you will need to choose a position for the stone lantern. If only one lantern is used in a tea garden, this should be placed to accompany the water basin, ostensibly to light the *tsukubai* arrangement and the path. In many Japanese gardens these lanterns are rarely lit – they are designed more for their artistic and sculptural quality. We have chosen the Oribe-style lantern, with a carved image of the Buddha on the pillar. This lantern is both easy to assemble and easy to install by burying the base of the pillar in the ground and securing it with concrete.

You will need
- a lantern set
- a spade
- a spirit level
- concreting sand or aggregate
- cement
- a shovel
- water for concrete and cleaning
- mastic (optional)
- low-voltage electrical supply (optional)

1 Lay out all the parts of the lantern to show the correct sequence of assembly. This lantern arrived from the supplier with pencilled-on numbers. Notice the rough granite base on the main lantern pillar: once the lantern is buried, this rough area will be covered.

2 Dig a hole to accommodate the base of the lantern. This should be 15cm (6in) wider than the base of the pillar and 10cm (4in) deeper than the height of the pillar that is to be buried.

3 If the base of the lantern is small, for example just 15cm (6in) deep, you will need a wider concrete base to make it more secure. Prepare a concrete mix made up of one part cement to six parts of concreting sand or aggregate. Add enough water to the mix to make a firm concrete. (A sloppy, wet mix will make it difficult to level the pillar base.) Place a shovel or two of the concrete mix in the hole.

4 If you are intending to light the lantern, thread an electric wire through the base before you lower the pillar into the hole. With the pillar in the hole, stand back and check that the front of the pillar is facing in the right direction. Using a spirit level, check that the pillar is standing vertically straight. If not, adjust it before the concrete sets.

5 Now check that the pillar is level horizontally by placing the spirit level across the top. After making any adjustments to the pillar position, check the level once again both vertically and horizontally until you are happy that it is straight.

6 With a concreting trowel, smooth concrete around the base, making sure it slopes away, and that no concrete will show once you have levelled the soil around it.

7 Leave the concrete mix to set for at least six hours before you add the remaining parts of the lantern. It is vital that the base is held firm before more weight is added.

8 Add each remaining part of the lantern in turn. Their weight gives them stability, but for absolute safety, secure the individual parts with some mastic.

9 Once the main box for the light is in place, position the two final elements: the roof of the lantern and the carved top.

LANTERN PRACTICALITIES

The following information will help you create an effective lantern feature:

• pick predrilled granite lanterns so an electric light can be inserted easily;

• ensure that you have a safe source of electricity (preferably low-voltage);

• LED lights consume little electricity.

Right: *In time, this lantern will weather and develop a surface of algae and moss.*

Laying stepping stones

The popularity of stepping stones in all Japanese gardens comes as a result of their introduction into the tea garden centuries ago. The stones themselves can vary in size and shape but are mostly natural and very thick, sometimes even whole rocks buried with just their tops showing. You can add formal paving, millstones or the occasional large stone beside the *tsukubai* or in any good place to stop and look around. Very large stones can lie on the ground just on a bed of sand, while smaller stones may need to be more firmly installed on a bed of concrete.

When planning a stepping-stone path, avoid using very smooth stones, as these can become slippery and dangerous, especially in damp shady areas. Naturally riven paving is safer and much more attractive to look at. Growing moss between the paving stones is the best approach for a Japanese garden to give the stone a distressed, timeworn quality, or alternatively you can try growing a few ground-hugging plants such as dwarf ophiopogon or ajuga to soften the paving edges.

You will need
- sharp sand
- a wheelbarrow
- a shovel
- a rake
- paving stones
- a sack truck
- cement (optional)
- a concreting trowel
- a rubber-headed hammer
- a spirit level
- a stiff broom

Above: *Stepping stones in Japanese gardens are often very thick and substantial, and are designed to sit proud of the surrounding area of gravel or moss.*

PATH DESIGN

Design your stepping-stone path as a weaving line of stones. This will add mystery to the garden as the path leads through the wilderness, past shrubs, trees and hills, towards the tea house itself.

1 Choose the line that your tea path will take and remove a layer of topsoil at least the depth of your stones. Collect some sharp sand in a wheelbarrow and pile it along the path. Use a generous amount – the eventual depth needs to be 4–7.5cm (1½–3in).

2 Spread the sharp sand along the path, ensuring it is flat, and even it out. Move the paving stones into place at the side of the path, preferably using a sack truck. You may need two people to handle any heavy, awkward stones.

3 Lay out the pattern of stepping stones before you finally set them. Stand well back from the pattern to assess the effect. In fact, it is advisable to leave them for an hour – even a day – and come back to look at them afresh. Then walk along the path to check that it is an easy and interesting route. Stones should be laid no more than 20cm (8in) apart, and at a regular distance from each other.

4 Heavy stones can be set directly on to the sand, but lighter stones will need a cement base. Make up a dry mix of eight parts sharp sand to one part cement. A dry cement mix is easier to use. Make four or five piles of the mix, 4–6cm (1½–2½in) higher than the desired height of the base of the stone.

5 Lower a paving stone on to the piles of cement. With the rubber hammer, tap the stone down until it is in position. Thin stones can easily break if not well bedded down. Repeat with the remaining stones.

6 The edges and corners of the stones are the most liable to break and tip over because they will take the pressure if the stone is unevenly supported, so shore up any hollow corners with some wet mix.

7 On a flat site, check the level of each stone, or if you are aware of the overall fall of the path, make allowances for this. If you don't have a spirit level, use builder's string laid along the length of the path, or you can simply lay a long length of timber down to make sure there are no snags that could trip someone up. Check the level from one stone to the next.

8 Brush sharp sand between the stones and wash the path down. This helps to eliminate air pockets, settle the sand and set the mix.

Right: *Plant around the paving or spread fine gravel or cobbles. To encourage moss, spread a thin layer of sharp sand, 2cm (¾in) deep, and press firmly into the soil.*

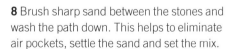

STROLL GARDENS

A stroll garden is one in which the visitor is encouraged to amble slowly along paths that circle a small pond or lake. Although there had been stroll gardens in Japan since the 14th century, they came to the fore in the Edo period of the 17th century and beyond. Unlike the earlier pond and stream gardens, where the emphasis was on the water, and boating was the main activity, the focus in a stroll garden was on the paths that wound among a new set of garden motifs. Classic examples are all large gardens, but, as long as there is room to wander, smaller ones are possible.

Although stroll gardens can include many elements, the individual components should not distract from the whole. The plan can simply include a path, a pond, a few clipped shrubs, a lantern and some trees, such as maples, pines or cherries. Decorative elements such as plants or statues should be used with care and restraint.

Even though stroll gardens may lack the spirituality of other styles, they obey certain rules of balance, and look to nature or famous scenes for their inspiration. When planning a garden in this style, focus on a simple design that includes a well-shaped pond and an interesting path, rather than an assorted handful of artefacts.

Above: *Recycled materials* (mitate) *such as these millstones make beautiful stepping stones for a stroll garden.*
Left: *The stroll garden at Murin-an is full of illusions – the two streams appear like great rivers flowing through "hills" of azalea.*

The stroll garden style

A stroll garden, just like a pond garden, should be set around a pond as its main feature. The pond is usually stocked with fish and circled by a winding path. The garden should be designed to be seen from various vantage points along this path, where special views are composed. These views can be of a single well-placed pine tree or of a whole scene of the pond with small hills beyond it, maybe with trees that act both as a backdrop and to frame a "borrowed view" or *shakkei* (using elements outside the garden).

ELEMENTS OF A STROLL GARDEN

A stroll garden is made up of many of the elements of pond gardens, dry gardens and tea gardens: a pond, a dry area, lanterns, buildings, fences or statues and decorative planting.

Pond

The garden should have a pond with a varied outline, or one that might correspond to a Chinese ideogram for water or heart. The inlet to the pond may include an area for water irises.

Dry area

An area between the main building and the pond can be made of sand, rocks and clipped shrubs. It can also include a tea arbour, stepping-stone paths, lanterns and water basins.

Above: *Stroll gardens usually had large ponds as the focus of the garden. Fishing pavilions such as this one would have been used for boating parties. It would also have given attractive views of the pond from the paths around the garden.*

Below: *Stroll gardens evolved in the Edo period, and incorporated many aspects of earlier styles. Paths circulate around the garden arriving at points with specially contrived views.*

Above: *Paths can be narrow or broad, cobbled or gravelled and may pass groups of trees.*

Right: *Most stroll gardens circle around ponds that are crossed by bridges, such as this one made with a curved stone.*

Lanterns

These can also be placed on the side of slopes or beside the pond – wherever makes the most pleasing composition.

Structures and statues

A rustic wisteria arbour, handsome stretches of bamboo fence, pagodas and statues of Buddha may all feature.

Plants

The planting can be varied and have something for every season. Many stroll gardens include a grove of cherries, but if space is limited, a single tree will do.

How to make a stroll garden

The stroll garden evolved as a style to combine many aspects of the tea garden, dry garden and pond garden. The central feature is usually a pond, with a gravel path that weaves around it, wandering through the garden and reaching vantage points to view specially composed scenes. Stroll gardens can range dramatically in size from park-like gardens to relatively small spaces; in small gardens, it may be possible to increase the sense of space using the technique of *shakkei*. The layout shown below is suitable for a reasonably large garden. A gravel path leads to a tea house, then over some stepping stones to a planted area almost surrounded by the pond. A wisteria has been trained over an arbour here and the trailing purple flowers reflect attractively in the water. The process of making this garden is shown in the following pages.

Above: *A path's "flow" is linked to the quality of the surface. Smooth gravel or neat granite pavers will enable easier movement than uneven, narrow paving stones. But the latter can contribute to the atmosphere of the garden.*

Wisteria arbour

Natural stone steps

Japanese red pine

Tea house

Stepping stones

Pond

Iris ensata   Lantern   Rocks around the edge

Ferns   Gravel path   Hydrangea

Right: *Tully Japanese Garden in Ireland has many features typical of an authentic Japanese stroll garden: a circular path, a pond, a tea arbour and a wisteria-clad arbour.*

PLANNING AND VISUALIZATION

To plan a stroll garden you need some kind of vision of a scenic landscape so that you can sketch out the general contours and outline of the pond. From the house you may also compose a scene that will be framed by a window or an arbour. In a stroll garden you may have some open grassy areas, some hills, a bridge and one or two good vantage points from where a variety of scenes can be viewed. Ponds should have some shady, deeper areas for fish to shelter from the heat. Paths can be made in any style but the main strolling path should be surfaced in gravel and wide enough for two people to be able to stroll side by side.

THE POND AND PLANTING

The main challenge is how to keep the pond water healthy. Unless you are lucky enough to have a natural stream, you will need to circulate the water with a pump. Drainage will be necessary to collect the overflow. You will need to be sure you can keep an adequate water supply going so that the water will be well aerated, so get advice on the size of pump required. Otherwise you might have a stagnant, half-empty pond by midsummer.

Make sure that your site is large enough to spread out the soil that is removed when you dig out the pond. This soil can be used to construct small hills, making the site more interesting and intriguing for people using the main gravelled path to wander around visiting tea houses and arbours.

Any fairly open site with good soil, some sunshine and good access can be used. Shady areas can be adapted to grow azaleas and hydrangeas, but cherry trees need an open aspect to grow and flower well. Wisteria too needs at least half a day in full sun to flower abundantly.

TYPICAL FEATURES OF A STROLL GARDEN

- a pond;

- a stream and cascade or waterfall;

- stone or wooden bridges over the stream or to an island on the pond;

- rocks among the plants on pond edge;

- small hills with dwarf or pruned pines;

- a strolling path in gravel or paving stones;

- gates into the tea garden;

- stepping-stone or paved tea paths;

- a wisteria arbour;

- a waiting room or bench;

- a tea house or tea arbour for viewing;

- fences surrounding the garden and bordering the tea path;

- shakkei, or "borrowed scenery";

- lanterns;

- water basins near tea house and on path;

- a dry garden near the house or in an enclosed courtyard;

- extensive plantings including: groves of cherries, plums and maples; groups of clipped azaleas, bamboo and hydrangeas; evergreen trees, especially pines, cryptomeria and hinoki cypress; herbaceous plants such as grasses, anemones, tricyrtis, platycodon, asters.

Making a pond with a flexible liner

The versatility of flexible (butyl) liners has made them the most popular of materials for a variety of applications for holding water, such as lining ponds and streams, and for backing around waterfalls. They certainly provide the greatest scope for small pond design. (For larger ponds, you will need to use a clay or synthetic clay liner; see pages 14–15.) They can also be used with natural stone, concrete or walling blocks to stabilize the sides of an excavation and have the advantage that they will not dry and become brittle if the water level should drop in dry weather.

Above: *When laying out a pond with a butyl liner, make sure that the liner is not visible, especially around the edges of the pond.*

To calculate the liner size, measure a rectangle to enclose the pool. After measuring the length and breadth, measure the depth and add twice that measurement to each dimension.

The measurements for length and width represent the minimum of liner required. Add about 30cm (12in) to each measurement to provide a small overlap of 15cm (6in) on each side. For brimming pools, where the surface of the water has to be level with the edge, add a little more than the width of the paving or bricks that will edge the pool to provide enough liner to extend beneath and behind (the end of the liner will finish by being held vertically behind the edging material).

One rectangle of liner can be used for a variety of pool shapes, including designs with narrow waists. Where the wastage would be excessive for narrow sections, smaller joining pieces of some types of liner can be welded together or taped together on site using proprietary waterproof joining tapes. Large creases in the corners of rectangular pools or sharp curves in informal shapes are inevitable, but they can be made to look less conspicuous if the liner is carefully folded before the pond is filled.

You will need

- a garden hose, rope or sand
- a spade
- plastic sheet
- a rake
- a spirit level
- a straight-edged piece of wood
- sand or underlay
- flexible liner (calculate the dimensions as described above)
- bricks or heavy stones as temporary weights
- large scissors
- paving for the pool surround
- ready-mixed mortar
- a mortaring trowel

1 If the pond is to be sited in a lawn, remove the turf by stripping off the grass to a depth of 5cm (2in) in squares of 30cm (12in) and stack the turf upside down for later use. Dig out the hole to a depth of 23cm (9in), angling the sides of the hole slightly inwards. The soil from the top 23cm (9in) can be stored on a plastic sheet nearby if it is to be used for any new contouring of the surrounds. Rake the hole base to a rough level finish after the first layer of soil has been removed and mark with sand the position of any marginal shelves around the sides.

2 The inner or deeper zone, avoiding the marginal shelf outlines, can now be dug out to the full depth of the pond. The soil from this deeper zone will be subsoil and can be used later if it is placed underneath any fresh topsoil. It should not become mixed with the freshly excavated topsoil. Marginal shelves around the sides of the hole should be 30cm (12in) wide and be positioned where you anticipate having the shallow water plants.

3 Rake the bottom of the pool to level the surface and remove any sharp stones, protruding roots or sharp-edged objects. Gently firm the surface by patting. Line the pool with about 1cm (½in) of damp sand – it should stick to the sides if they slope slightly. If the soil is stony, drape a piece of underlay across the hole and shelves, to overlap the edge of the pool by about 30cm (12in).

4 Lay the flexible liner over the sand or underlay. Once you have done this, place temporary weights, such as bricks or heavy stones, on the edges of the liner to keep it securely in place. Make sure that there is enough liner width above the edge of the pool all the way round. Then use a hose to start filling the pond with water.

5 Wait until the water has almost filled the pool, then remove the bricks or stones temporarily holding the edges of the liner. Replace any turf you want around the edge, and complete any edging finishes before the water is filled to the final level. Trim the surplus liner only when you are completely sure that the water level and edging are working satisfactorily.

6 Cut away the surplus liner and underlay, leaving an overlap around the edge of about 15cm (6in) to be covered by the paving.

7 If you want edging paving, bed the paving on mortar, covering the edge of the liner. The paving should overlap the edge of the pool by about 2.5cm (1in). Finish off by pointing the joints with mortar using the mortaring trowel.

8 If there is ample surplus liner, features such as bog gardens can be made around the sides. When a kidney-shaped pool is created, a small bog area can be achieved using the corner piece of a rectangular liner. Instead of cutting off the surplus, place soil on the liner and prevent it from spreading into the main pool water by a small submerged retaining wall of inverted turfs, rocks or walling stones.

Right: *This small pond is surrounded with gravel and provides a home for koi carp.*

Making a gravel path

The Japanese stroll garden is specially designed for taking a walk around the scenic environment and for this you will need a suitable path. A gravel path may seem simple to make, but it must be done properly or all sorts of problems will ensue. The edging of gravel paths is vital, as it prevents the gravel from drifting on to beds, grass or mossy areas. In Japanese gardens this edging is often made of stone or granite blocks. When choosing suitable blocks you should always aim to achieve a balance between the natural and the artistic.

Above: *The minimum width of a path for two people to stroll side by side is 1.5m (1½yds). As well as this practical role, paths also play an important part in linking garden elements and creating fluidity in the design.*

The most common mistake made by gardeners is to dig out a trench and fill it with pea gravel. However, deep gravel is very spongy, making it awkward to walk on, and almost impossible to push a wheelbarrow or wheelchair over. For a successful path, follow the guidelines below.

You will need
- a spade
- a shovel
- a rake
- a wheelbarrow
- edging stones
- concreting sand and cement
- a concreting trowel
- a rubber-headed hammer
- weed-suppressing landscape fabric
- scissors
- "scalpings" or a mix of crushed stone and stone dust
- gravel
- a roller or motorized wacker plate

1 Mark out the edges of the gravel path you are planning. Using a shovel, dig out the area of the path down to a depth of 10–15cm (4–6in) and remove the soil. Lay out the edging stones informally.

2 Position the stones so that you can see what they look like before you actually fix them in place.

3 Fix the edging stones in place using a concreting mix of one part cement to eight parts sand. Firm them in place with a rubber hammer and check that they are level.

4 The concrete mix on the inside edge should fall below the stones by at least 4cm (1½in). Allow the concrete to set for a day before proceeding. Collect some soft sand in a wheelbarrow and bring it to the path.

5 Lay a thin layer of soft sand over the path area. This will protect the landscape fabric from being punctured by small stones.

6 Lay out the landscape fabric so that it tucks in around the edging stones. Cut the fabric to shape with sharp scissors.

7 Spread a layer of "scalpings" or crushed stone/stone dust mix to a depth of 10–12cm (4–5½in), raking it evenly so that the top level is 2–4cm (¾–1½in) below the top of the edging stones. Do not roll this layer.

8 Spread a single layer of gravel over the "scalpings" base, and rake it out evenly.

9 Roll the single layer of gravel so that it is pressed well into the base layer. Now spread another single layer of gravel over this pressed surface and roll again. (Do not spread more than 4cm (1½in) of gravel in total. You can always top it up later.) Test the surface for firmness and comfort before adding any more gravel. Rake out the gravel around the edges of the path so that it works in nicely around the edging stones.

GRAVEL OPTIONS

Type of gravel	Advantages	Disadvantages
Very fine gravel	Easy to deal with, attractive to look at	Can get caught in the soles of shoes and can easily be kicked around the garden
Sand/stone mix	Gives a firm, well-drained finish	Expensive
Stone chippings	Attractive and interesting to look at	Can be uncomfortable to walk on in soft-soled shoes
Pea gravel 10–20mm (½–¾in) in diameter	Ideal for general use, beds down well and tends to stay in place	Will need raking and topping up from time to time

Below: *Gravel paths should be raked and brushed regularly to keep an even layer of gravel.*

Making a wisteria arbour

The native Japanese wisteria, *Wisteria floribunda*, can be seen cascading out of trees on hillsides and valleys in some parts of Japan. Wisteria is ideal for festooning wooden arbours, constructed so that the long scented flower racemes hang down between the rafters. The pendulous flowers look especially wonderful when reflected in water, so arbours are often constructed near to or even leaning out over ponds. In Japan, wisteria arbours are very simple constructions that can be easily assembled from round poles or branches with the bark still on them.

Although rustic poles are ideal for an arbour, it is sometimes difficult to find ones of sufficient strength. (Indeed, some arbours are built using concrete "logs".) This project gets around this problem by using square posts and beams locked together using mortise-and-tenon joints that are fixed by a dowelling peg. The rafters can then be made of rustic poles laid across the beams or lighter-weight poles can be simply fixed in place with screws.

Above: *The two most popular species of wisteria are* W. floribunda, *the Japanese species with very long racemes, and* W. sinensis, *the Chinese species whose flowers are half the length. You will need to allow plenty of headroom in an arbour for these trailing flowers to hang.*

You will need

- posts and beams, 10–14cm (4–5½in) square, made of green oak, cedar or treated softwood
- rafters, 7.5–10cm (3–4in) in diameter, made of rustic poles
- a post-hole digger
- a crowbar
- a spade
- concreting aggregate and cement
- metal post fixers (optional)
- a hammer and chisel to make mortise-and-tenon joints for the upright posts
- 10mm (½in) diameter dowelling
- an electric drill and 10mm (½in) wood drill bit for dowelling
- 7.5cm (3in) screws

1 Mark on the ground where the arbour posts will be placed, making sure they are square.

2 Dig the post holes 25cm (10in) wide and 4cm (1½in) deeper than the post will be. The posts should be set at least 45cm (18in) deep if set in concrete. Make sure the posts are upright and in line.

3 Lightly nail the rafters at an angle from one post to another to make the structure secure.

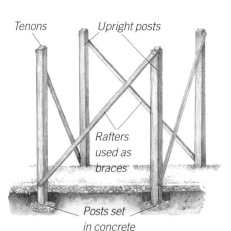

4 Set the posts in a concrete mix of one part cement to six parts concreting aggregate. The rafters should ensure that the arbour stays square as the concrete sets. This process requires precision.

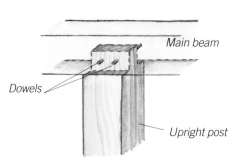

5 Lay the main beams on the mortise-and-tenon joint uprights (at the top of the posts). From the side, drill twice through the beam and the tenon of the post, and hammer in two lengths of dowelling.

6 The dowelling should be tight but it will swell up and tighten more once it gets wet. Set the holes around the posts in the same concrete mix that was used in step 4, ensuring the joints line up snugly, and leave the structure to set for at least 24 hours. You may need to adjust the joints during this time, especially if you are using green oak, which can warp quickly. Once the concrete is set, further bending of the oak will add to the pergola's natural charm.

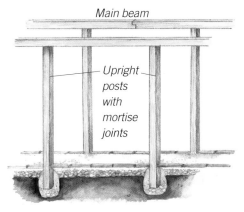

7 Remove the brace rafters. Rest the rafters on top, across the main beams. They can be notched to fit over the beam to hold them in place. One or two screws drilled from above down into the main beams should fix them. The arbour is now ready as a structure over which wisteria can be planted and trained.

ARBOUR DESIGN

Timber A mature wisteria plant has twisting stems that can exert a stranglehold on any structure, so any timber you use must be of sufficient strength and thickness to withstand its grip. Green oak is both strong and long-lasting.

Height Japanese wisteria flowers can be more than 50cm (20in) long, so the roof of the arbour should be high enough for a person to stand in comfort beneath the flowers – a recommended 2.5m (8ft).

Posts Set the posts no more than 2m (6½ft) apart along the sides, and at least 1.5m (5ft) apart across the width of the path.

Fixings You could construct an arbour using screws, bolts and nails, but it may not last as long as a mortise-and-tenon jointed construction.

Joinery You may be able to ask a timber merchant to cut the pieces of wood for you and to make the mortise-and-tenon joints. It will then be simply a case of assembling the arbour.

Above right: *This sturdy wisteria arbour draws the viewer into the garden. Arbours are best placed at transition points in a garden.*

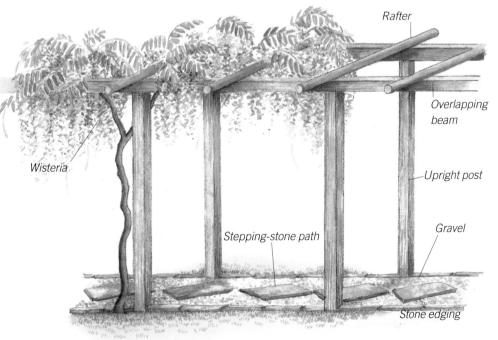

Rafter

Overlapping beam

Upright post

Gravel

Wisteria

Stepping-stone path

Stone edging

EXTENDING A BEAM

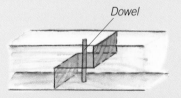

Dowel

If the main beam requires extending to give the arbour the length you require, create an L-shaped notch in the two pieces of wood, and secure with wood glue. Then drill a hole through both parts and insert a dowelling rod through. When the wood becomes wet, the dowel will tighten.

COURTYARD GARDENS

The history of the courtyard garden starts in the early 17th century, but for contemporary designers the small, enclosed space adjoining a building still offers fantastic design possibilities. The design is generally simple, sometimes planned as a light extension to the house with large windows and doors, sometimes as a usable outdoor space. Small courtyard gardens, designed to be viewed through glass panels or set within atriums open to the sky, are now being created everywhere from large museums and corporate headquarters to private homes.

The versatility of the courtyard garden means that it can provide anything you want it to. It can be a dry garden, a tiny tea garden, a miniature landscape, an area that encapsulates nature as a motif, or even a tranquil contemplative space. The courtyard garden can be both a retreat from the busy streets outside and an opportunity for escapist fantasy.

In its design, the courtyard garden absorbs the best of Japanese culture, where one often sees one art form impacting on another, showing how the courtyard garden itself is an art form that is constantly evolving.

Above: *Tall water basins* (chozbachi) *are often placed where they can be reached from the veranda.*
Left: *This tiny courtyard garden at Sanzen-in is a welcome island of green in the centre of the building.*

The courtyard garden style

The form of a courtyard garden has many variations. The main criterion is that it is a small, sometimes minuscule, space contained within a building or the narrow passage that leads from a street to the main door of the house. The courtyard might be viewed from more than one room, so it should look good from more than one angle and is an excellent opportunity to experiment in miniature landscapes or with abstract design, mixing the many elements that make up the various styles. You may find this style of garden in a Japanese restaurant, a hotel or even a temple garden.

ELEMENTS OF A COURTYARD GARDEN

Most courtyard gardens are dry gardens, often laid out with a spread of gravel, sometimes with a stepping-stone path crossing over it. Although the space is limited, there may be room for a very small pond, but in courtyards where no soil is available and light is poor, a purely "dry" garden is ideal.

Lanterns and water basins, along with minimalist planting, are key features.

With enough space, you could combine rocks and plants, a waterfall and a small pond, but more often a courtyard may have only enough space for an island of greenery in the middle, decorated simply with a few rocks, ferns, a water basin and lantern.

Above: *A chequered pattern of moss and gravel on the Brunei Gallery roof garden in London evokes the one used by Mirei Shigemori at Tofuku-ji in the 1930s.*

Below: *Dry gardens suit roof gardens well, where the weight of soil and invasive plant roots might damage the building. This dry courtyard garden contrasts natural rock forms with carved blocks.*

Lanterns and water basins

Most courtyard gardens include a lantern and water basin arrangement, similar to that found in a tea garden. A taller water basin, or *chozubachi*, can also be placed where it can be easily reached from the veranda of a nearby room or passage, and where the eaves of the house help to protect the water.

Plants

In a very shady courtyard, some plants do not grow well, and you will have to choose shade-loving plants such as aucuba, camellia and bamboo. With more light, a single pine tree or cherry tree might provide a point of focus and possibly some welcome shade in the heat of summer.

Left: *These raised paving stones give a sculptural quality, as well as leading up to the veranda.*

Below: *Courtyard gardens can be made in almost any enclosed space. They are typically bordered by the walls of the house.*

How to make a courtyard garden

The courtyard garden is any small area in an enclosed space that incorporates traditional features found in other Japanese garden styles. Some are dry gardens with just a spread of sand and one or two rocks, while others might include elaborate paths that cross over the space, using plantings that evoke a distant but miniaturized landscape. Here is a suggestion for a courtyard garden in a level space. A mound (middle back), which represents a hillside, is planted with a dwarf Japanese red pine, ferns and *Ophiopogon japonica*. The space itself is walled on one side and has a bamboo screening fence on two other sides. Crossing the space is a semi-formal stone path leading from a door in the house to a side gate. Like most courtyard gardens, this one also includes a lantern and a water basin – elements borrowed from the tea garden. The process of making this garden is shown on the following pages.

Above: *Defined as a closed-off external area, the courtyard garden is an excellent style to use for controlled drama. The minimalism and simplicity of this design, a view from a Japanese restaurant, creates an attractive, peaceful pictorial composition of the enclosed garden beyond.*

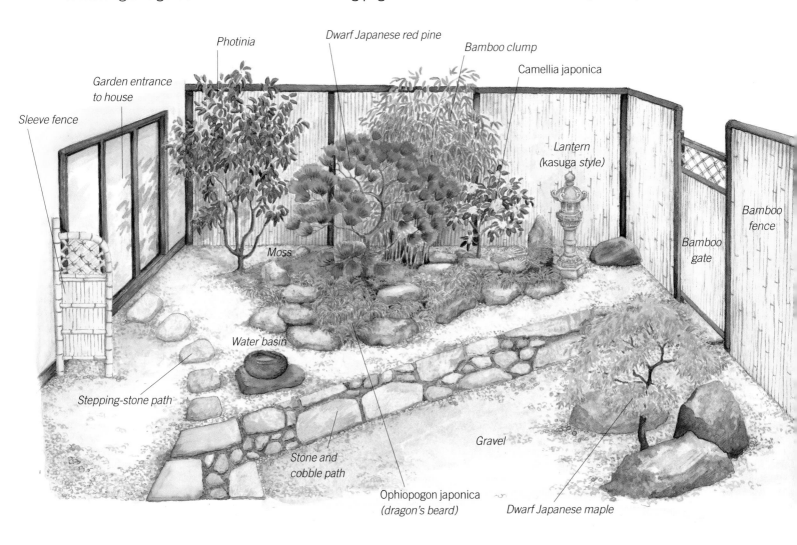

Photinia

Dwarf Japanese red pine

Bamboo clump

Camellia japonica

Garden entrance to house

Sleeve fence

Lantern (kasuga *style*)

Bamboo fence

Bamboo gate

Moss

Water basin

Stepping-stone path

Stone and cobble path

Ophiopogon japonica (dragon's beard)

Gravel

Dwarf Japanese maple

COURTYARD GARDEN: TYPICAL FEATURES

The following features would normally be found in a courtyard garden:

• sliding screens, small fence panels and bamboo blinds for private areas;

• dry-garden elements with one or two rocks and a "pool" of raked gravel;

• stone paving bordered by lanterns;

• stepping stones;

• clipped evergreens such as azaleas, mahonias, nandinas and bamboos;

• glossy evergreen shrubs, such as aucubas, fatsias and camellias, as well as shade-loving ferns, bamboos and farfugiums;

• a carpeting of moss;

• lanterns, basins and small bridges.

PLANNING AND VISUALIZATION

Before making a courtyard garden, you need to think carefully about your design. If you want to include a number of features, then you must have an overall composition that is coherent. Is your garden going to act as a path from one room to another, or is it simply going to be viewed from one or two points?

Your next consideration is a question of scale. A *shakkei*, or condensed landscape, for example, should not have too many features, as this might make it appear too busy. Make a plan, and stand back from time to time to check the view over the garden as you construct it.

As courtyards are, by their very nature, enclosed, access to them can be tricky, so make sure you can get all the materials into the space (some may have to come through the house, which could be difficult). Also, being so close

Above: *This courtyard garden was designed to be viewed from more than one angle and to act as a passage to a back gate. The path then becomes an intrinsic part of the design.*

to a house, the space may have water, electricity and gas services crossing underneath, so check before doing any excavation. Generally, deep excavation is not necessary in courtyard gardens except to ensure that the site is well drained before planting anything.

Courtyards may not have a great deal of light, so plants should be carefully chosen to suit the amount of light available. Remember that you will need a source of water to irrigate the plantings, to maintain any water feature and to keep the space clean. Electricity may be required for lighting or for any water pumps, but neither of these is essential for a successful courtyard garden.

Building a bamboo screen fence

The design and construction of bamboo fences in Japan has developed into a highly specialized and elaborate art, and if you are interested in developing the skills to make your own traditional fence, there is no shortage of information available. If you prefer a more instant solution, however, you can buy sections of these beautiful bamboo fences ready-made from specialist suppliers. In this project, rolls of bamboo canes, held together with wire and supported with a frame, were used, which required a fence on two sides that would act as a screen.

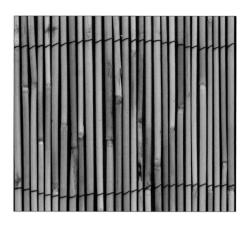

When using bamboo in rolls, you will need to build a suitable frame against which to support the bamboo. Every one of the timber elements in the frame should be made of durable hardwood or treated softwood. You should also remember to apply an additional coat of preservative to the parts of the posts that are going to remain underground.

Above: *A detail of bamboo fence supplied in a roll. This economical form of fencing is often used, even in authentic Japanese gardens. Bamboo of this type will usually need replacing after five to ten years, depending on the weather and how well it is cared for.*

You will need

- 10cm (4in) square posts, 2.5m (8ft) long
- a 5 x 7.5cm (2 x 3in) supporting baton, ideally just one length measuring the length of the fence
- temporary supporting batons to hold posts in position
- 4 x 5cm (1½ x 2in) cross batons, in 1.5m (5ft) lengths
- capping timber 14 x 4cm (5½ x 1½in), the length of the fence
- vertical strips 2.5 x 7.5cm (1 x 3in) and 2m (6½ft) long for facing boards to hold the fence in place
- a roll of bamboo fencing, 2m (6½ft) high – these are usually available in 3m (10ft) lengths
- a wood saw
- an electric drill
- 6cm (2½in) screws
- a screwdriver
- a spirit level
- concrete mix of aggregate using 1 part cement to 6 parts aggregate
- a chisel
- a shovel
- a wheelbarrow
- thick black jute twine

1 Identify your fence line with builder's twine. Mark out the position of the posts, around 1.5–2m (5–6½ft) apart. Dig holes for the posts up to 45–50cm (18–20in) deep by 20cm (8in) wide. Stand the posts upright in the holes. Screw on the lower supporting baton, which should be 4cm (1½in) off the ground and perfectly level. This will help to keep the posts square.

2 For extra stability, erect some temporary supporting batons to help hold the posts perfectly upright while the concrete sets.

3 Make up a mix of concrete and fill the holes, tamping it in firmly around the posts. Using a spirit level, check again that the posts are in line, and are square and upright. Leave the concrete to set for at least 24 hours.

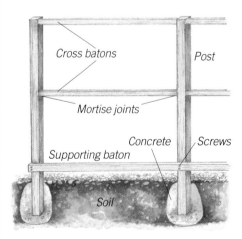

4 Once all the posts have set, remove the temporary supporting batons. Chisel out shallow mortises in the uprights to receive the cross batons (see mortise-and-tenon detail shown on page 54). The cross batons, and therefore the joints, should be positioned half way up the posts and at the top of the posts. From the side, drill through and screw the mortise-and-tenon joints into the posts.

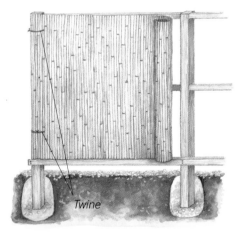

5 Stand the roll of bamboo fencing on the lower supporting baton, temporarily attaching one end of it to a post with some twine. Unroll the fence, attaching it to the cross batons with twine as you go and as necessary to hold it in place. You can leave the twine in place attaching the bamboo roll to the cross batons as additional support, particularly if you weave it in a way that makes it an attractive addition to the design.

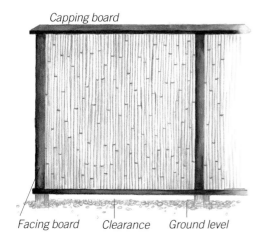

Capping board

Facing board *Clearance* *Ground level*

6 To hold the bamboo roll securely in place, screw facing boards on to the posts. Cut off the tops of the posts so that they are level with the top of the bamboo fence roll. Lay the capping boards over the tops of the posts and then screw them down on to the posts. Either stain all the exposed timbers ash black or leave them to weather naturally.

Below: The neutral colour and quality of bamboo fences make them excellent backdrops to many styles of Japanese garden.

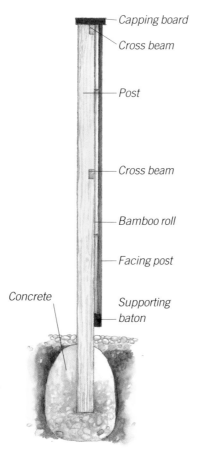

Capping board

Cross beam

Post

Cross beam

Bamboo roll

Facing post

Concrete

Supporting baton

MAINTAINING THE FENCE

If you maintain your bamboo fence well, it will last much longer. Bamboo will eventually become brittle and attract mould if left untreated, so, every year or two, scrub off the mould and apply either some light teak oil or a matt varnish diluted 1 part varnish to 3 parts white spirit. (There are special wood preservatives formulated for willow and hazel fences that would be equally effective on bamboo.) To make maintenance easy, make sure that you attach the bamboo roll to the fence in such a way that it will be easy to remove. For example, don't use heavy nails as these will be hard to pull out without damaging the frame.

Note that some bamboo rolls are made of heavier cane than others – the larger the cane, the longer they will last.

Left: Cross-section of a bamboo fence.

Laying a paving-stone path

There are many styles of stone path to choose from in the Japanese garden, but they almost all use natural materials in a combination of formal and informal shapes. Your choice of design may be determined by the availability of materials. This courtyard garden uses a combination of local paving stones, most of which have at least one straight edge, and large cobbles from a local quarry. Using the straight edge to act as a border to the path, the cobbles are set out to weave a thread through the path, unifying the design.

Above: *A randomly paved path makes a bold entrance to the Huntington Botanical Gardens. The guardian dogs are a Chinese inspiration.*

It is advisable to lay a path with a complex design such as this on a level site over a concrete base. You should make sure that the surface allows rainwater to drain off, because stones that stay wet will become slippery and therefore dangerous.

To keep the stones clean, lay them on a dry mix of cement and moist sand, rather than using a wet cement mix. This mixture can also be easily brushed into joints between the stones. The mixture will then set either from the moisture in the sand or from rain. If the weather remains dry, hose down the paving stones with water after they have been put in place to make sure that the cement sets properly.

There is a danger of the stones becoming stained by the cement while laying. For any persistent stains, use a stain remover, such as muriatic acid, which will dissolve cement. Always follow the manufacturer's instructions carefully when using chemicals.

You will need
- hardcore for the base
- a wheelbarrow
- a sack truck
- different sizes of natural paving stones
- large rounded cobbles or smooth, flat-topped stones
- marker paint or powdered lime
- white chalk
- concreting sand and cement
- a shovel
- a tape measure
- a bricklaying trowel
- a rubber-headed hammer
- a stiff broom
- stain remover (muriatic acid)
- old rags
- builder's twine

1 Prepare a level site with a solid hardcore base and lay out the stones and cobbles on the ground to establish the pattern you want. Mark out the outline of the path with marker paint. This type of paint comes in spray cans, and is available from most builders' merchants. Alternatively, sprinkle a line of powdered lime which will dissolve after a few days.

2 Number or code each stone with white chalk so you remember which stone goes where in the path. Then remove all the paving stones to one side of the path. Obviously some variations may occur when you replace the stones, but try to keep the main dynamic of the design within the marked eges of the path.

3 Dig out the base to a depth of 10–16cm (4–6¼in), allowing 5–7.5cm (2–3in) for the concrete mix and 3–5cm (1¼–2in) for the paving thickness, and 2–4cm (¾–1½in) for the gravel. If you want the paving to sit proud of the ground, reduce the depth to allow for this.

4 Make a mix of 1 part cement to 8 parts sand. Lay the paving slabs first, spreading this mix (dry or wet) to a depth of 5–7.5cm (2–3in).

5 The mixture should be heaped up in the corners so that each stone is laid higher than its intended level, as its weight will press the mix down.

6 Once the stones have been laid and the mortar mix is set, fill in over the mortared areas with a dry mix of 1 part cement to 8 parts sand and brush it level. Tamp the stones down gently with the handle of a hammer. Use a spirit level to check that the stone is level.

7 Lay out the cobbles on top of the dry mortar mix, push them down and tamp them into position. Here, the cobbles sit proud of the mortar mix, which has hardened from the ambient water and some rain.

8 Once the stones and cobbles have nearly set, apply some water to the surface to check it flows away from the path. Brush or scrape out any excess mortar that may be preventing water from draining off the surface of the path.

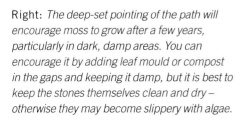

9 After two or three days, wash off any stains from the path using stain remover and a rag.

Right: *The deep-set pointing of the path will encourage moss to grow after a few years, particularly in dark, damp areas. You can encourage it by adding leaf mould or compost in the gaps and keeping it damp, but it is best to keep the stones themselves clean and dry – otherwise they may become slippery with algae.*

Building a mound

Courtyards are often contained on level sites within buildings or compounds where there is little or no soil, and where a complex web of underground services may be running beneath the garden. In this courtyard garden, building up a mound of earth answered this practical issue, and also added to the artistry of the garden, because the mound of earth takes on the representation of a landscaped hill, or even a mountain. Planted with a dwarf Japanese red pine, and laid with rocks, the garden has the feeling of a condensed landscape.

As moss can be tricky to establish in many climates, planting the lower level with dwarf ophiopogon helps to give the appearance of a grassy hillside, while ferns soften the outline of the rocks. Finally an authentic Japanese touch is achieved by placing both a lantern and a water basin just off the paved path that crosses the courtyard to the gate.

Above: *Mounds of moss represent the Mystic Isles in this courtyard garden. Rocks in a large expanse of raked sand complete the picture. The mounds form dramatic shapes in the space and give structure and balance to the created landscape.*

You will need
- 2–3 tonnes of screened topsoil
- a wheelbarrow
- a shovel
- a selection of small rocks
- a sack truck to move rocks
- plants: a dwarf Japanese red pine, a clump of *Ophiopogon japonicus*, a *Camellia sasanqua*, two *Polystichum setiferum* (ferns)
- a planting trowel
- a paving stone
- sharp sand
- a rubber-headed hammer
- a water basin
- a lantern
- gravel
- a rake
- a broom

PRIOR PLANNING

- Assess the site access before ordering materials such as soil and rocks.

- If you are building a mound on a rooftop, ask a building engineer to assess the load that the building can carry.

1 Add a heap of screened topsoil to the area, surrounding it with a ring of stones to prevent soil spilling on to the gravel. The stones can be moved later, so put them into temporary positions for now. Then start shaping the mound so that it has natural contours.

2 Plant large shrubs first. Placed at the highest point, the dwarf Japanese red pine anchors the mound, accentuates the shape of the hill and gives a central feature. Place more rocks on the banks of the mound to create the escarpments and rocky outcrops.

3 Partly bury the rocks so that only a third remains exposed. Simply placing rocks on top of the soil will look unnatural. Reshape the mound and build up soil behind the rocks for planting pockets and to create a more uneven shape. Stand back to check the result.

4 If you already have a clump of ophiopogon or have bought a large pot, you can divide the plant up by simply pulling it apart. Firmly gripping the base of the plant, tease it apart gently, taking care not to break too many of the roots.

5 Plant your ophiopogon divisions around the slopes of the mound at a distance of approximately 15cm (6in) apart, tucking them under the rocks. The plants will spread until they knit together eventually to form a carpet. Plant the ferns underneath the pine.

6 The next stage is to lay a well-shaped paving stone on to which you will place the water basin. The paving stone can be simply laid on a bed of sharp sand, without any cement. Spread the sand out evenly and then raise it up in small ridges.

7 Lay the stone on the sand base. Tamp the stone down with a rubber-headed hammer.

Below: The underplanting of Japanese mondo grass (Ophiopogon japonicus) will knit together to form a solid carpet over the next few years.

8 Place the water basin on the stone. Leave space at the side for a ladle, for guests to drink from and clean themselves.

9 Follow the step-by-step guide to installing a lantern on pages 40–41. Place some more rocks artistically around the lantern and in other places on the flat area.

10 Spread an even layer of gravel over the entire flat area to create a dry garden effect. Clean the paving and brush out any gravel that has strayed into the joints of the paving.

PLANT DIRECTORY

The Japanese have planted beautiful trees and shrubs ever since they first started making gardens. Although initially many plants were brought over from China, gardeners soon harnessed the potential of the native plants. Japan has exceptional and enviable flora, including many species of cherry, azalea, camellia and magnolia, which blossom in the mountains in spring, while in the autumn, maples and oaks give a display of fiery reds, yellows and oranges. Evergreen trees such as cedars and pines are considered symbols of longevity and resilience.

Wisterias, peonies and hydrangeas feature in many Japanese gardens, in natural groupings or massed in orchard-like groves rather than in formal beds. Herbaceous and bulbous plants, such as platycodons, lilies, hostas or Japanese anemones, are usually planted naturalistically with ferns in individual clumps near the base of a rock, in a carpet of moss, or scattered in small groups. Irises are grown in swampy areas or in formal beds near the inlet of ponds, while sedges and ferns are used to soften the edges of streams. This chapter will show you many of the best plants to use, along with seasonal highlights and care instructions.

Above: *The stunning autumn foliage of* Acer palmatum *'Sango-kaku'*.
Left: *Wisteria is a classic plant in Japanese gardens.*

Spring trees & shrubs

The first signs of spring are a cause for celebration throughout the temperate world, but especially in Japan. In spring gardeners enjoy the bright green of new buds and the blossoms of the azaleas. Camellias and some azaleas are evergreen; some varieties flower very early, and they lend themselves well to being clipped. Kerria has been grown in Japanese gardens since the 11th century and often flowers early, as do many species of magnolia, some of which are native to Japan. You will also find many varieties of rhododendron in full bloom.

Above: *The red flowers of* Chaenomeles japonica, *the Japanese quince, open almost as soon as the winter ends.*

Camellia japonica
Tsubaki

Camellia

Family: Theaceae

This evergreen shrub, native to the warm temperate coasts of Japan, is planted in gardens together with species and hybrids from China. *Camellia sasanqua* has smaller, narrower leaves than *C. japonica*, and the pale pink single flowers appear sporadically through winter before dropping when spent.

Camellias are now common, but in the past they were found mainly in Buddhist temples. The simpler, paler coloured, single-flowered forms with glossy foliage, known as *wabi-suke*, were planted in tea gardens. Two types of camellia can be grown as hedges: the dense, glossy foliage of *C. japonica* or the tea plant *C. sinensis*, with smaller leaves than other species and white flowers in autumn, often clipped to give a compact, dense shape.

Propagation semi-ripe leaf cuttings
Flowering time mid- to late spring
Size shrub or small tree to 10m (30ft); keep to 2m (6½ft) by restricting the roots in a tub, or by regular stem pruning
Pruning by thinning out stems after flowering
Conditions light shade and away from early morning sun; moist, acid soil
Frost hardy/Z 6–7

Chaenomeles japonica
Boke

Japanese quince, japonica

Family: Rosaceae

The Japanese quince, or japonica, is loved for its early spring flowers, which range in colour from the deepest scarlet to pale pink and white. They appear before the leaves, clustered close to the bare, spiny stems. It can be pot grown, when it tends to take on a wizened habit of growth.

Propagation semi-ripe cuttings
Flowering time spring
Size shrub to 1m (3ft)
Pruning by cutting back hard after flowering to encourage a compact habit, or training against a frame or wall
Conditions sun or partial shade; well-drained, slightly acid soil
Fully hardy/Z 5–8

Kerria japonica
Yamabuki

Jew's mallow

Family: Rosaceae

A deciduous shrub native to Japan, kerria has been grown in gardens since the 11th century. Its simple, five-petalled, orange-yellow, star-like flowers are a welcome sight in spring. The double-flowered form is most common in the West, but Japanese gardens tend to use the single form, usually planted as part of a broad scheme.

Propagation hardwood cuttings
Flowering time mid- to late spring
Size shrub to 2m (6½ft)
Pruning by thinning out old stems after flowering
Conditions full sun or partial shade; any soil
Fully hardy/Z 5–9

Camellia japonica

Kerria japonica

Magnolia

Magnolia spp.
Mokuren

Magnolia
Family: Magnoliaceae
Native magnolias have been planted down the centuries and include the deep purple-pink, lily-flowered *Magnolia liliflora*, known as mokuren; the familiar white, star-flowered *M. stellata*, hime-kobushi; and its taller close relative, *M. kobus*, kobushi. The large *M. obovata*, to 15m (50ft), is a hardy, deciduous tree with highly scented, cream-coloured flowers in midsummer. In more recent years the bold American evergreen species, *M. grandiflora* (bull bay), growing to 18m (60ft), has proved popular, with its large, cream-coloured flowers appearing in late summer. Magnolias are usually planted in large stroll gardens.
Propagation seed and grafted
Flowering time mid-spring to midsummer
Size large shrub or small tree, 3–12m (10–40ft)
Pruning by removing over-long shoots in late winter; best left unpruned
Conditions partial shade; rich, acid soil
Fully to frost hardy/Z 5–9

Paulownia tomentosa
Kiri

Foxglove tree
Family: Scrophulariaceae
Although strictly a native of China, the foxglove tree has been cultivated in Japan since the 9th century. Planted as specimen

trees in the courtyard gardens of aristocrats, they became associated with the military leader, Hideyoshi. Paulownias have two notable features: the fabulously large leaves and the beautiful, lavender-blue, foxglove-shaped flowers. It may take a few years and some mild winters before a *Paulownia* will establish a strong stem, but once a trunk has been developed, the tree will form a handsome and perfectly hardy crown.

Alternatively, the stems may be coppiced in spring to encourage the production of massive leaves, up to a metre (40in) wide. This eliminates the flowers, but when combined with bamboos, palms and cycads, it has a bold, tropical look.
Propagation seed
Flowering time mid- to late spring
Size tree to 12m (40ft)
Pruning none needed unless grown as a pollard
Conditions sheltered position in full sun; any soil
Frost hardy/Z 6–9

Rhododendron spp.
Satsuki (small-leaved); hirado (large-leaved)

Rhododendron, azalea
Family: Ericaceae
Evergreen and deciduous azaleas belong to the genus *Rhododendron* (Tsutsuji), of which 50 species are native to Japan. The two main kinds of azalea are the kirishima (*R. obtusum* type) and the slightly later flowering satsuki (*R. indicum*). There is also the large-leaved azalea, called hirado. Most of the

thousand or more hybrids are of mixed parentage and have flowers that span the colour spectrum from purple to pink, salmon and white. Flower sizes vary, as does the growth.

Azaleas, most of which flower after the cherries and wisterias, have no symbolic significance in the Japanese garden. Kirishima azaleas have been grown in gardens since the 11th century, though they are often seen on treeless mountainsides in drifts and mounds. This natural habit has made azaleas the perfect subject for clipping for centuries; they lend themselves to being rounded into mounds that imitate hills, trimmed down to echo the shape of a stream, or used in a clipped form with rocks or at the edge of small pools to add shape and contrast. The clipping also reduces the number of flowers, which, to the Japanese, is a bonus because too much colour over-stimulates the senses. Left unclipped, their flowering is so profuse that the leaves are completely obscured.

The art of *o-karikomi* (similar to the representational forms of topiary) is often practised on blocks of azaleas and camellias. In the garden at Shoden-ji, three groups of clipped azaleas have been planted as part of a dry landscape (*kare-sansui*).
Propagation seed, softwood cuttings
Flowering time spring to early summer
Size shrub 1–3m (3–10ft)
Pruning by shaping after flowering and, if necessary, again in the autumn
Conditions full sun or shade; moist, acid soil
Fully hardy to frost tender/Z 6–9

Paulownia tomentosa

Rhododendron

Spring blossom

The end of winter is signalled by the plum blossom (mume) whose flowers, appearing as the last snows melt, are regarded as brave and resilient. The delicate pink flowers of the peach tree (momo) are the next to open after the plum, but it is for the sakura or cherry blossom that Japanese gardens have become famous the world over. Indeed, their first flowers entice people out to celebrate spring. Cherry trees are relatively shortlived and are only lightly pruned, while the longer-lasting plum is tolerant of hard pruning.

Above: *The kikuzakura (chrysanthemum cherry), flowering in late April/early May, has as many as one hundred petals per blossom.*

Prunus mume
No-ume
Japanese plum or Japanese apricot
Family: Rosaceae
Like the European sloe (*Prunus spinosa*) and the damson (*P. damascena*), the deciduous Japanese plum has a pure white blossom, which may open in some areas while snow is still on the ground. The earliness of the blossom makes it one of the most popular flowers in Japan. The flowers of some forms are pale or deep pink, covering whole valleys with a haze of colour. The round fruit is often pickled or candied.

Unlike cherry trees, which are relatively short-lived and resent being pruned, venerable plum trees may be pruned hard. Old trees with their branches covered in lichen are revered more than vigorous young trees; the gnarled trunks might need to be propped up and bandaged like an old soldier, with ropes, jute and hessian, and should still bear a few branches with blossom.

The festivals of plum-blossom in Japan lack the boisterous aspect that you often find later in spring under the boughs of cherry blossom. Plum blossom appears when the weather is often quite cold and is viewed with quiet solemnity, touched with a hint of sadness. A symbol of purity and hope, it is revered as the prophet of spring. *Prunus mume* is also seen as the epitome of integrity and fidelity, "as virtuous as a true gentleman", and its resilience marks it out as one of the "three excellent plants" that bear the winter so bravely (the others are pine and bamboo). It was said to be a courageous tree, releasing its scent from leafless branches while the last of the winter cold persists, which is why it was popular with warriors, who might carry sprigs of plum blossom into battle. According to Japanese legend, when a warbler (the equivalent of a nightingale) sings in the branches of the plum tree, the two join together to become the spirit of the awakening spring.

The most common variety of *Prunus mume* in cultivation in Western gardens is the deep pink form called 'Beni Chidori',

Prunus mume

which is sweetly scented. It is an upright shrub to 3m (10ft). The variety 'Omoi-no-mama' is white. Suitable substitutes for damsons include *P. cerasifera* (cherry plum, myrobalan), which grows to 10m (30ft) and has white flowers in early spring (but avoid the purple-leaved form, 'Nigra'); *P. cerasifera* 'Princess' is suitable for a small garden. *P. glandulosa* is a shrub, to 1.5m (5ft), with white to pale pink flowers followed by red fruit.
Propagation budded or grafted
Flowering time early spring
Size small tree to 9m (9yd)
Pruning by thinning out old stems after flowering
Conditions full sun; any soil
Fully hardy/Z 7–9

Prunus persica
Momo
Peach
Family: Rosaceae
The deciduous Japanese peach is the next flowering tree, after the plum, to be honoured in spring. Peaches were planted in great numbers on the sides of Kyoto's Momo-yama (Peach mountain) as an emblem of longevity and perfection. It was on this same mountain that the great shogun Hideyoshi built his Fushimi castle in the late 1500s; his reign was later referred to as Momoyama.

Prunus persica

Peach blossom is a soft, vibrant pink, and the flowers appear just as the leaves unfurl. The peach was thought to win over the spirits of the dead, and was also a sign of new life. Concoctions of peach were taken at the first sign of pregnancy and were administered as a cure for morning sickness. Peach blossom festivals, originating in China, are still celebrated at the beginning of March. They are a special favourite with children, especially girls, who decorate themselves and their dolls in silk and lacquer.

Peach trees are generally rather short-lived (as little as 15 years) and are prey to a number of pests, including the disfiguring peach leaf curl.

Propagation budded or grafted
Flowering time early spring
Size tree to 8m (25ft)
Pruning by removing dead, diseased and damaged branches in midsummer
Conditions full sun; rich, well-drained soil
Fully hardy/Z 7–9

Prunus serrulata
Sakura
Japanese cherry
Family: Rosaceae
It is for the sakura, or cherry blossom, that Japanese gardens have become famous the world over. Their first flowers bring people out in celebration, and there are huge spring festivals for three weeks in April. The length of Japan, "The Land of the Cherry Blossom", friends gather in gardens and public parks to have picnics and sip sake well into the night, as the ephemeral clouds of blossom float above them. People also tie red paper lanterns in the branches, while children run around in the early evening, clapping to the music of drums and *shamisens*, a lute-like instrument.

The classic Japanese cherries mostly date from the late 19th-century Meiji period. These trees often have fully double and profuse blossoms that derive from the Japanese hill cherry, *Prunus serrulata*. The best-loved forms are those with white flowers and dark, unfurling leaves that are revealed as the petals fall.

Before the 19th century Japanese gardeners mainly grew the species *P. incisa* (Fuji cherry), *P. serrulata* (the Japanese hill cherry) and *P. jamasakura* (formerly *P. serrulata spontanea*), when their more subtle elegance was in keeping with the aesthetics of the times. These trees were the object of veneration and celebration, their short-lived blossom being viewed by the samurai as a reminder of their own fragile mortality, and a symbol of chivalry and loyalty to their lords and masters.

The first of the cherries to flower, from late autumn to spring, is *P.* x *subhirtella* (Higan cherry, rosebud cherry). Its weeping forms, 'Pendula Rosea' and 'Pendula Rosea Plena', are very popular in Japan, the cascading branches being propped up by cedar poles and bamboo frames. *P. incisa* flowers soon after, just before its leaves appear, and makes a small, spreading, attractive tree to 8m (25ft), ideal for the smaller garden.

The next to flower is the hybrid *P.* x *yedoensis* (Yoshino cherry), which is named after Mount Yoshino. The white flowers appear just as the leaves break from their buds, and the spreading tree has a lovely, weeping form, 'Shidare-yoshino'. Around the Arishyama district of Kyoto and the gardens of the Tenryu-ji, hundreds of Yoshino cherries have been planted and admired for over 800 years.

The foliage of *P. incisa* also turns beautiful shades of yellow, orange and red in autumn.

In the last 200 to 300 years, especially during the early 19th century Edo period when plant breeding became very popular in Japan, innumerable hybrids and forms of *P. serrulata* were raised. These have become known as simply "Japanese flowering cherries" or Sato zakura (literally "domestic cherries").

Japanese flowering cherries are very easy to grow in almost any soil type that is neither too wet nor too dry. The roots are often very shallow, sometimes lifting to the surface. In general they are short-lived trees, some living less than 50 years. They do not flower all at the same time, so it is possible in a large garden to make a selection from these hybrids and the other species that extend the flowering season from very early spring to late spring.
Propagation budded or grafted
Flowering time early to late spring
Size tree 3–8m (10–25ft)
Pruning only by removing dead, diseased and damaged branches in midsummer
Conditions full sun; rich, well-drained soil
Fully hardy/Z 7–9

Prunus x yedoensis

Late spring & summer trees, shrubs & climbers

As the last of the cherry blossom falls, the wisteria unravels its pendulous, perfumed flowers. Alongside the wisteria, the tree peony unfurls its fabulous frilly petals. This is a plant with sumptuous flowers, which was highly regarded by the Chinese long before the Japanese introduced it to their gardens. Other plants are grown for their shape and foliage as much as for their flowers, and small trees such as *Styrax japonicus* (Japanese snowbell) continue their blossom season into the summer. Clematis are popular in Japan but are mostly grown in pots.

Clematis spp.
Tessen
Clematis
Family: Ranunculaceae
Some species of large-flowered clematis, such as *C. patens*, are native to Japan. The colourful hybrids of *C. patens* are often planted in containers near the main entrance.
Propagation seed, all cuttings, layers
Flowering time summer
Size climber up to 4m (13ft)
Conditions sun and part shade
Fully to half hardy/Z 4–9

Cornus kousa
Mizuki
Japanese flowering dogwood
Family: Cornaceae
A handsome deciduous large shrub or small tree up to 10m (33ft) with wide spreading tiered branches that carry flowers with four white bracts in early summer. They open green and change to pure white, or pink in the variety 'Satomi'. *C. k.* var. *chinensis* freely bears larger and whiter flowers than the straight species. *C. k.* and its forms are outstanding – hardy and grown in most soil types, they also flower in midsummer. There are some hybrids between this species and the American flowering dogwood, *C. florida*, which flowers earlier in the spring.

    C. k. and *C. florida* both turn tones of red and purple in the autumn, keeping their display for up to a month.

Clematis patens

Propagation grafted, layers, seed or softwood cuttings
Flowering time early summer
Size small tree to large shrub, to 10m (33ft)
Conditions sun or part shade
Fully hardy/Z 5–8

Cornus kousa

Above: Deutzia gracilis. *This small shrub is smothered with flowers in late spring and has an attractive fine texture.*

Deutzia spp.
Unohana, utsuki
Japanese snowflower
Family: Philadelphaceae
The Japanese grow many species and forms of deutzia. The white or pink flowers are borne later than those of other spring-flowering shrubs. *D. crenata* and *D. gracilis* have clusters of star-shaped white flowers.
Propagation stem cuttings
Flowering time late spring to early summer
Size shrub 1m (3ft)
Pruning by cutting out old flowering stems after flowering
Conditions full sun; any reasonable soil
Fully to frost hardy/Z 5–9

Paeonia suffruticosa
Botan, moutan
Tree peony
Family: Paeoniaceae
Known as the "king of flowers" because of its luxuriant blooms, the tree peony is not easy to cultivate in Japan, and the flowers are rather too gorgeous and blowsy for the subtle refinement of most of their gardens, so it is usually grown in pots. The most prized colours are white, pale pink and red. It is often represented on painted screens.

Spiraea nipponica

Propagation grafted
Flowering time late spring to early summer
Size shrub to 2.1m (7ft)
Pruning by removing over-long and crossing shoots in late winter
Conditions full sun or partial shade
Fully hardy/Z 4–8

Sophora japonica
Enju

Japanese pagoda tree
Family: Papilionaceae
This fine stately tree, growing ultimately to 20m (65ft), has elegant pinnate leaves and produces large panicles of small white flowers in late summer.

In Japanese gardens you will often see the weeping form *S. j. pendula*, which needs support as even its main stem has a serpentine nature. The tree may become self-supporting, making an umbrella-shaped mound.
Propagation seed (weeping form is grafted)
Flowering time late summer to autumn
Size medium-sized tree up to 20 (65ft)
Conditions sun
Fully hardy/Z 7–9

Spiraea nipponica
Shimotsuke

Nippon spiraea
Family: Rosaceae
Several species of spiraea are native to Japan. They make a round or spreading shape, with arching growth, decked with bunches of tiny flowers. *S. n.* has dark green leaves and white flowers.
Propagation semi-ripe cuttings
Flowering time midsummer
Size shrub to 1.2m (4ft)

Pruning cut hard after flowering
Conditions full sun; any soil
Fully hardy/Z 5–9

Stewartia pseudocamellia
Hatsutsubaki

Japanese stewartia
Family: Theaceae
Grown for its small, white-cupped, camellia-shaped summer flowers, mottled bark and autumn tints, this small to medium tree is often planted among mixed blocks of evergreens or as a specimen near a gateway.
Propagation seed
Flowering time midsummer
Size tree to 20m (65ft)
Pruning none needed
Conditions full sun or light shade; moist, acid soil; does not tolerate wind or drought
Fully hardy/Z 5–7

Styrax japonicus
Storax

Japanese snowbell
Family: Styracaceae
A small deciduous tree, with glossy, dark green leaves and masses of white flowers.
Propagation seed
Flowering time early to midsummer
Size tree to 10m (30ft)
Pruning none needed
Conditions full sun or partial shade; moist, neutral to acid soil
Fully hardy/Z 6–8

Ulmus parvifolia
Akinire

Chinese elm
Family: Ulmaceae
This graceful medium-sized tree has small leaves and hop-like flowers late in the summer. Some dwarf forms, such as 'Yatsubusa' and 'Hokkaido', have extra dense growth and very small leaves.
Propagation seed (dwarf forms cuttings)
Flowering time late summer to autumn
Size medium-sized tree up to 20m (65ft)
Conditions sun
Fully hardy/Z 4–8

Wisteria spp.
Fuji

Wisteria
Family: Papilionaceae
Once the cherry blossom has fallen, the long racemes of wisteria unravel. *W. floribunda* has longer racemes than *W. sinensis*, and in 'Macrobotrys' the racemes can reach 1.2m (4ft) long. Wisterias are planted on frames, arbours and tripods or draped over a bridge. *W. brachybotrys* 'Shiro-kapitan' (syn. *W. venusta*) produces scented white flowers. Suitable for pot growing and bonsai treatment.
Propagation mostly grafted, seed
Flowering time early summer
Size to 9m (30ft)
Pruning in midsummer and in midwinter
Conditions full sun or partial shade
Fully to frost hardy/Z 4–10

Sophora japonica

Wisteria

Summer flowers

Japanese summers often bring heavy rain, which few flowers can endure. However, hydrangeas continue to flourish in these conditions, and in recent years they have gained in popularity. Apart from hydrangeas, two flowers are often grown as Buddhist symbols of mortality and immortality: the annual morning glory for its fleeting existence, and the lotus, a symbol of purity as it emerges out of the wet mud in ponds. The iris is also planted in or near water, and is a plant celebrated for its power to ward off evil spirits.

Above: *The mop-headed* Hydrangea macrophylla *here grows profusely in a shaded woodland.*

Hydrangea spp.
Ajisai
Hydrangea
Family: Hydrangeaceae
Hydrangeas were first mentioned in Japanese gardens as early as 759, but they did not become instantly popular. The four petals and rather gloomy purple colours were thought to represent death. The common name, ajisai, means "to gather purple". They were also called shichihenge, which meant "to change seven times", alluding to the way in which the flower colour changes through the season.

Three of the most important species of hydrangea are native to Japan, *Hydrangea macrophylla, H. petiolaris* (climbing hydrangea) and *H. serrata*. The great round mop-head hybrids originated here and are found in a number of Japanese gardens. Among their useful attributes are their late-summer flowering and their ability to withstand heavy summer downpours. On acid soil with plenty of moisture, the blue varieties are intensely blue. The lacecaps, which come closer to the species in their flower form, are also very elegant and suitable for planting in light woodland shade, where their mysterious beauty can be almost bewitching, especially when the flowers are moist from the rain. Varieties of *H. macrophylla* can be grown in pots, if regularly fed and watered. The other species that is native to Japan is *H. paniculata*, which has cone-shaped flowerheads in late summer. It is ultra-hardy and can be grown in full sun. All these hydrangeas come in a multitude of forms to suit every taste, and they have become very popular in Japan in recent years, with some towns and districts making the hydrangea their special flower.
Propagation semi-ripe and hardwood cuttings
Flowering time mid- to late summer
Size shrub to 2m (6½ft)
Pruning by removing dead and over-long shoots in early spring
Conditions sun or partial shade; moist, rich soil
Fully to frost hardy/Z 4–9

Ipomoea
Asagao
Morning glory
Family: Convolvulaceae
During the Nara and Heian periods, when poets typically sang of the fleeting condition of human life, they latched on to morning glory as an ideal symbol: as one flower fades after a day of glory, it is quickly replaced by another. But it was in the 18th and 19th centuries that the morning glory became fashionable among the *daimyos*, who helped to create a new array of colours. Morning glory is usually grown in pots over lightweight bamboo trellises and fences. While so many flowers tend to wilt at the onset of summer, the morning glory revels in the heat.
Propagation seed
Flowering time summer to autumn
Size climber to 6m (20ft)
Conditions full sun; any soil
Half hardy to frost tender/Z 8–10

Hydrangea

Ipomoea

Iris laevigata

Iris spp.
Hanashobu
Iris

Family: Iridaceae

The iris is a great favourite in Japan. *Iris laevigata*, known as kakitsubata, grows naturally in the swamps around the ancient capital of Nara, where it was collected to be made into a dye, its blue colour exclusively used to decorate the robes of the imperial family. In *The Pillow Book*, a novel dating from the 11th century, the author writes of the iris festival when men, women and children warded off evil spirits by adorning their hair and clothes with iris flowers and roots. The festival still takes place in late May and early June.

I. laevigata is cultivated in gardens in swampy, but not waterlogged, ground, often near an inlet to a pond. *Yatsuhashi* or zigzag plank bridges weave over the beds, forcing the visitor to slow down and admire the plants from different angles. The flowers are said to have a "naive neatness" that needs no improvement; they are narrower and smaller than the larger and flatter *I. ensata* var. *spontanea*, known as hanashobu.

Hanashobu is more spectacular than kakitsubata and has been bred intensively. It now comes in all shapes and colours, from white and pink to deep purple, and is often cultivated in large beds in slightly ridged rows or in pots, so that it can be admired as an individual against golden folding screens.

In parts of Japan where they cannot cultivate either of these irises for lack of water, the European *I. germanica* is often grown in the same way, in large beds exclusively devoted to irises. Other irises grown are *I. tectorum* (roof iris) and the shade-loving *I. japonica*, whose wild look is perfect for the tea garden.

Propagation division
Flowering time summer
Size to 80cm (32in)
Conditions full sun or partial shade; slightly acid soil
Fully hardy/Z 4–9

Nelumbo nucifera
Hana-basu
Lotus

Family: Nymphaeaceae

By high summer the glories of the spring blossom have long faded, and it is time for the lotus to bloom. The lotus is the flower most closely associated with Hinduism and Buddhism, and the Buddha is often portrayed in statues and images sitting on a lotus, in his state of perfect enlightenment. The lotus symbolizes the evolution of the human spirit, with its roots in the mud, its growth passing through water and air and into the sun, to open, pure and unsullied. The wheel-like formation of the petals is also said to represent the cycle of existence.

A succession of flowers opens over six weeks, the buds opening at dawn with an indescribable sound. The white flowers of *N. nucifera* 'Alba' have an especially powerful and sweet perfume. Lotus flowers close in the heat of the day and after a couple of days gracefully fall, one petal at a time, leaving their distinctive honeycombed seed pods. The lotus is also an important source of nourishment. The seeds, roots and leaves are all eaten, but varieties grown as food rarely flower. The lotus is not reliably hardy, and some climates are simply not hot enough in the summer to stimulate its flowering. In these circumstances *Nymphaea* (waterlily) is a good substitute, although the flowers sit closer to the surface of the water and are not held on erect stalks, like the tall flower stems of the lotus.

Propagation division
Flowering time summer
Size 1.2m (4ft) above water
Conditions in full sun; in water to a depth of 60cm (24in)
Frost tender/Z 4–11

Iris ensata

Nelumbo nucifera

Autumn foliage

Plants that celebrate autumn with their colourful leaves were known collectively as *momichi*, but in time the term became synonymous with the beautiful tones of *Acer palmatum*, the first entry here. Traditional Japanese gardens do contain other trees and large shrubs, although the *Acer* varieties will always be favourites for autumn colour. Some of these trees and shrubs also turn beautiful colours in autumn, while others are more valued for their glossy evergreen leaves as a foil to the bright foliage of the *Acer* and other plants. A few are scented or bear edible fruits.

Acer palmatum
Kaede
Japanese maple
Family: Aceraceae
The Japanese love to view the flaming autumn tints of the Japanese maple. There are hundreds of fancy types, some with finely cut leaves and others with variegated and purple foliage. *A. p.* is the chief focus of all the celebrations in gardens and in the wild. *A. micranthum*, *A. tataricum* var. *ginnala* and *A. japonicum* all turn beautiful colours, but in November the temples and gardens of Kyoto are ablaze with the fiery red and orange leaves of *A. palmatum*. Some very beautiful forms have foliage that is salmon-tinted in spring, while some turn bright yellow rather than red in autumn, and others have bright red or green stems in winter. The dwarf and cut-leaf forms may be more suitable for the smaller garden, but avoid the purple-leaf forms, which distract from carefully composed, harmonious arrangements.

Acer palmatum 'Linearilobum'

Propagation seed and grafted
Size small tree to 8m (25ft)
Pruning best left unpruned; can cut out over-long stems in late winter
Conditions full sun or partial shade
Fully hardy/Z 5–8

Other species of maple, native to Japan:

Acer buergerianum
Buerger-kaede
Trident maple
Family: Aceraceae
This small oval tree is often seen in larger gardens. In a mild autumn it holds on to its leaves well into the winter, and will not always colour reliably. It has a multi-stemmed habit and medium-fine, glossy dark green leaves.

Acer cissifolium
Mitsude-kaede
Ivy-leaved maple
Family: Aceraceae
This barely looks like a maple at all with its three-lobed leaves. It is one of the first to colour in autumn, but keeps those leaves for a remarkably long time as they turn a patchwork of oranges, yellows and reds.

Acer ginnala
Amur-kaede
Amur maple
Family: Aceraceae
An upright but eventually broad spreading small tree that has handsome leaves. The form *A. ginnala* 'Flame' has been selected for the brilliance of its autumn colours.

Above: Acer palmatum *can be grown as a single or multi-stemmed small tree. Its leaves turn to shades of scarlet, yellow or orange.*

Acer japonicum
Momji
Full moon maple
Family: Aceraceae
Second only in popularity to *Acer palmatum*, *A. j.* has much larger leaves. Rarely grown in gardens it has produced the two forms of 'Aconitifolium' and 'Vitifolium', bold and fine plants which are easily grown, slowly becoming medium-sized trees. 'Vitifolium' has leaves like grape vines while those of 'Aconitifolium' are deeply incised. Both come into leaf very early and turn fiery red in autumn. The golden-leaf form is classified as *A. shirasawanum* 'Aureum'. Another form of this latter species is *A. shirasawanum* 'Ogurayama', with smaller leaves and a more upright habit. *A. sieboldianum* is similar to both these and makes a small tree.

Acer micranthum
Komine-kaede
Komine maple
Family: Aceraceae
A small-leaved maple that grows in native forests in central Japan with *Acer palmatum*. It forms a delightful small wide spreading tree that colours brilliantly in autumn.

Acer rufinerve
Uri hada kaeda
Redvein maple
Family: Aceraceae

This snake-bark maple has long white striations in the bark and beautiful leaves that turn a mix of yellow and red.

Cercidiphyllum japonicum
Katsura

Katsura tree
Family: Cercidiphyllaceae
This medium- sized tree has ascending branches and rounded leaves that colour up in the autumn. As the leaves fall they give off an aroma akin to burnt, sugar.
Propagation seed
Size tree to 20m (65ft)
Pruning by removing over-long or crossing branches in late winter
Conditions sun or light shade; slightly acid soil
Fully hardy/Z 5–9

Diospyrus kaki
Kaki

Persimmon
Family: Ebenaceae
An autumn tree with yellow to orange fruits. The most edible of date plums, it is grown for its eaves, which turn yellow, orange-red and purple before they fall. In cold areas this plant is best grown against a wall.
Propagation grafted
Flowering time summer
Size tree to 10m (33ft)
Pruning by removing over-long or crossing branches in late winter
Conditions sheltered site in full sun; rich soil
Frost hardy/Z 4–8

Acer cissifolium

Enkianthus perulatus
Dodan

White enkianthus
Family: Ericaceae
This large shrub has clusters of small cream- and pink-tinted bells in spring, but is more often grown for its bright red and golden-orange autumn foliage. When pruned hard it produces few flowers, although judicious pruning can enhance its tiered branching. Grow as a hedge or mix with evergreens. An alternative is *E. campanulatus*.
Propagation semi-ripe cuttings
Flowering time mid-spring
Size shrub to 2m (6½ft)
Pruning by cutting out crossing or over-long shoots in early spring
Conditions sun or partial shade; moist, slightly acid soil
Fully hardy/Z 5–7

Ginkgo biloba
Icho

Maidenhair tree
Family: Ginkgoaceae
The leaves of this ancient maidenhair tree, curiously shaped like webbed feet, turn to shades of bright butter yellow in autumn. Ginkgo is found all over Japan, especially in Kyoto, where trees grow to an immense size and smother the ground under them with blankets of yellow. They produce an edible but unpleasant-smelling fruit in autumn. *G. b.* 'Annie's Dwarf' is suitable for small gardens or pot culture.
Propagation seed and grafted
Flowering time (catkins) spring
Size tree to 30m (100ft)
Pruning by removing diseased or dead branches in late winter or early spring
Conditions full sun; any soil
Fully hardy/Z 5–9

Nandina domestica
Nanten

Sacred bamboo
Family: Berberidaceae
The nanten is a close relative of *Berberis*. In midsummer, small white flowers are carried in large open panicles, and they are followed by red berries. In a good autumn the leaves turn bright red, especially if the shrub has been planted in full sun. In very cold areas many of

Enkianthus perulatus

the leaves tend to fall by late winter, but the plant is considered to be evergreen.
Propagation seed
Flowering time midsummer
Size shrub to 2m (6½ft)
Pruning trim back over-long shoots in spring
Conditions full sun; moist soil
Frost hardy/Z 7–10

Stewartia pseudocamellia
Hatsutsubaki

Japanese stewartia
Family: Theaceae
Each leaf of this plant turns a mixture of yellow, orange, green and red. It also has small white flowers in high summer.
Propagation seed
Flowering time midsummer
Size tree to 20m (65ft)
Pruning none needed
Conditions full sun or light shade; moist, acid soil
Fully hardy/Z 5–7

Styrax japonicus
Storax

Japanese snowbell
Family: Styracaceae
This, combined with various cherries, adds lovely shades to the autumn garden. Its leaves are dark green and it bears masses of small white flowers in summer.
Propagation seed
Flowering time early to midsummer
Size tree to 10m (30ft)
Pruning none needed
Conditions full sun or partial shade
Fully hardy/Z 6–8

Autumn flowers

The "seven grasses of autumn" have been known and used in Japan since the 11th century. The selection of these seven herbaceous plants has varied over the centuries and from region to region, but in general they are the ones that flower after the summer rains and during the autumn leaf colour season. Included here are some of the original seven, together with a few others that have since gained in popularity. Except for *Miscanthus* none of these are grasses, and the remainder can be categorized as meadow flowers.

Above: *Potted hybrid chrysanthemums outside a Japanese temple.*

Anemone spp.
Shuumeigiku
Anemone
Family: Ranunculaceae
Plants known as Japanese anemones have been developed from the Chinese import *Anemone hupehensis*, which has been extensively hybridized. This tall herbaceous plant with vine-like leaves is often seen in shady gardens, planted in clumps of moss and beside streams. The finest form is the single, pure white *A.* x *hybrida* 'Honorine Jobert', but there are many cultivars, with colours ranging from white and pale pink to a deep purple-pink, some with double flowers. In fertile soil it can be invasive and may need to be kept under control.
Propagation division
Flowering time late summer to mid-autumn
Size perennial to 1.2m (4ft)
Conditions sun or partial shade; rich, moist soil
Fully to frost hardy/Z 5–8

Callicarpa japonica
Murasaki shikobu
Japanese beauty berry
Family: Verbenaceae
Named after the author of the great 11th-century novel *The Tale of Genji*, the Japanese species *Callicarpa japonica* (beauty berry) is a low-growing, arching, deciduous shrub, which bears beautiful purple berries in autumn and winter. It has delicate pink flowers that arrive in the early summer (which precede the purple berries) and simple, medium blue-green leaves. Its larger cousin, *C. bodinieri* var. *bodinieri* 'Profusion', is more frequently planted in Western gardens but is a much larger shrub.
Propagation semi-ripe cuttings
Flowering time late summer
Size shrub to 1.5m (5ft)
Pruning cut back close to ground level in early spring
Conditions sun or light shade; rich soil
Fully hardy/Z 5–8

Chrysanthemum spp.
Kiku
Chrysanthemum
Family: Asteraceae
Almost all chrysanthemums have now been reclassified as members of the genus *Dendranthema,* but most gardeners still use the old name. The plant was long associated with the imperial Japanese family, and its mythological status has made it the subject of fairy stories and legends. Extracts and essence of chrysanthemum were believed to possess miraculous powers for a longer life.

The large, ball-shaped flowers are rarely seen in Japanese formal gardens, but are often grown in pots, outside temples and in domestic gardens. Great pride is taken in the cultivation of the artificial giants, but more modest species are grown in gardens. The related *Leucanthemum* x *superbum* (formerly *Chrysanthemum* x *superbum*, shasta daisy), with white, yellow-centred flowers, like a large marguerite, might flower in late autumn. These, and a number of wild asters, are suitable for the wilderness parts of the tea garden.
Propagation cuttings and division
Flowering time early to late autumn
Size perennial to 1.5m (5ft)
Conditions sheltered position in full sun; rich soil
Fully to half hardy/Z 4–9

Anemone

Callicarpa japonica

Eupatorium

Eupatorium spp.
Fujibakama
Hemp agrimony (UK)
Joe Pye weed (US)
Family: Asteraceae
The Japanese species *E. chinense* and *E. lindleyanum* are tall herbaceous plants with flattened heads of fuzzy purple or white flowers, which are adored by bees. The subdued colouring and upright habit make them excellent for semi-naturalizing.
Propagation seed and division
Flowering time autumn
Size perennial 1–2m (3–6½ft)
Conditions full sun or partial shade; any moist soil
Fully hardy to frost tender/Z 4–9

Lespedeza bicolor
Hagi
Shrubby lespedeza
Family: Papilionaceae
The purple-flowered bush clover is a lax and arching shrub, which comes into leaf

Lespedeza bicolor

late in the season. Its purple, broom-like racemes of flowers, up to 15cm (6in) long, appear in autumn at the ends of shoots and side-shoots on wand-like stems 1–3m (3–10ft) long.
Propagation seed and division
Flowering time mid- to late summer
Size shrub to 2m (6½ft)
Pruning by cutting down to ground level in early spring
Conditions full sun; well-drained soil
Frost tender/Z 4–6

Miscanthus sinensis
Obana, susuki
Fountain grass or Eulalia grass
Family: Poaceae
Because *Miscanthus sinensis* colonizes waste ground in Japan it is rarely used as a garden plant. When it is, it is used with restraint. The silvery plumes, which appear in autumn, reach 2–4m (7–13ft) high. *M. sinensis* 'Yakushima Dwarf' is a low-growing form from Yakushima, the volcanic island off the south coast of Japan, which makes a rounded clump 1m (3ft) high and across. The old flower and leaf stems turn to shades of fawn, persisting into the New Year before being dispersed by the wind. Eulalia grass covers many of the hills in Japan, where it waves elegantly in the wind.
Propagation division
Flowering time autumn
Size grass to 4m (13ft)
Conditions full sun; well-drained soil
Frost hardy/Z 5–9

Platycodon grandiflorus
Kikyo, asagao
Balloon flower
Family: Campanulaceae
From the campanula family, the balloon flower has inflated and pleated flower buds that give the plant its name. The flowers, which eventually open to a wide cup, are mostly blue, but can also be pink or white. This compact, herbaceous plant with blue-green leaves will do well if planted near the edge of a stream.
Propagation seed and division
Flowering time late summer

Miscanthus sinensis

Size perennial to 60cm (24in)
Conditions sun or partial shade; moist soil
Fully hardy/Z 4–9

Tricyrtis
Hototogisu
Toad lily
Family: Convallariaceae
The old Chinese name for this plant means the "oil spot plant" because its flowers are freckled with maroon to purple spots. Its Japanese name, hototogisu, is the same as the name for a cuckoo, which has a freckled chest. This genus, known in the West as toad lily, has only recently become popular in Japan, where its wild forms with their modest and mysterious colours are suitable for planting in moist shade beside a tea garden path or near a stream.
Propagation division
Flowering time late summer to mid-autumn
Size perennial to 80cm (30in)
Conditions shade; rich, moist soil
Fully hardy/Z 7

Tricyrtis

Evergreen shrubs

Japan's flora is rich in native evergreen shrubs. Many are grown in and around the gardens of Kyoto. The following selection has been made for the plants' hardiness and general availability. Camellias and azaleas have already been discussed under spring-flowering shrubs (see pages 70–71), but they need to be mentioned again because they form the backbone of most evergreen schemes in Japanese gardens, especially as they can be well pruned and shaped. Many of these evergeen shrubs can be grown in the shade of trees and buildings.

Above: Buxus microphylla *var.* japonica *is a dense evergreen shrub that can be used to form small hedges and topiary.*

Ardisia japonica

Ardisia japonica
Senryo
Marlberry
Family: Myrsinaceae
Seen in many gardens in Kyoto and in the south of Japan, marlberry is a delightful evergreen shrub which is only hardy in sheltered spots. *Ardisia japonica* is a small shrub with white or pale pink flowers, which are followed by red or yellow berries. They last from autumn into winter.
A. crenata (coralberry, spiceberry), which is known as manryo, is a larger shrub, to 2m (6½ft), with white or pink flowers followed by scarlet fruits.
Propagation seed
Flowering time summer
Size shrub to 1m (3ft)
Pruning by removing over-long shoots in mid-spring
Conditions sheltered position in shade; moist, rich, acid soil
Frost hardy/Z 4–8

Aucuba japonica
Aoki
Japanese laurel
Family: Cornaceae
The spotted laurels are reliable evergreen shrubs with glossy foliage. They love shade and tolerate the dry soil among the roots of large trees. In the autumn female shrubs bear small clusters of large red berries, so they are sometimes called Japanese hollies. There are forms with yellow-spotted leaves and others with orange or yellow berries, but in Japanese gardens the most popular plant is the species or its narrow-leaved form, 'Salicifolia'.
Flowering time mid-spring
Size shrub to 3m (10ft)
Pruning by removing crossing or over-long shoots in late winter or early spring
Conditions shade or partial shade; any soil
Frost hardy/Z 7–10

Aucuba japonica

Buxus microphylla var. japonica
Asama tsuge
Japanese box
Family: Buxaceae
The Japanese box is a small evergreen shrub up to 2m (6½ft) high and wide. It is hardier than *Buxus sempervirens* (the European boxwood), and has longer, narrower leaves and a more compact habit. Many hybrids and forms exist in rounded, dwarf forms, such as 'Compacta' and 'Green Pillow'. It is easily grown in sun or shade. Like all box, this species can be clipped into almost any shape and this makes it an excellent plant for Japanese gardens, especially in soils of high alkalinity where azaleas are not able to grow.
Propagation hardwood cuttings
Flowering time spring
Size shrub to 2m (6½ft)
Conditions sun or shade
Fully hardy/Z 5–8

Cleyera japonica
Sakaki
Japanese cleyera
Family: Theaceae
This slow-growing evergreen shrub with upright rigid growth is sacred to the Shinto religion. Boughs of its scented leathery foliage are presented at special ceremonies and it is often planted near Shinto shrines and in gardens in Japan. *Cleyera japonica* is not fully hardy, so it should be grown in a sheltered spot on an acid soil.
Propagation seed, semi-ripe cuttings
Flowering time early summer
Size to 10m (30ft)
Conditions sun to light shade; moist, well-drained acid soil
Frost hardy/Z 8

Daphne odora
Jinchoge
Winter daphne
Family: Thymelaeaceae
This small evergreen shrub carries its deliciously sweet-scented, pink-white flowers in late winter to early spring. It is most often seen in gardens in the form 'Aureomarginata', which has gold-edged leaves, and is a lovely plant to include in a mixed planting, but is not very long-lived. Note: it is highly poisonous.
Propagation seed or semi-ripe cuttings
Flowering time late winter to early spring
Size shrub to 1.5m (5ft)
Pruning best left unpruned
Conditions sun or partial shade; rich, moist, slightly acid soil
Frost hardy/Z 8–10

Elaeagnus x ebbingei

Daphniphyllum macropodum
Yuzuri-ha
Family: Daphniphyllaceae
A handsome large-leaved shrub, bearing long strap-like leaves with red leaf stalks. This Japanese native plant, which can be grown in almost any moisture-retentive soil in sun or part shade, makes a good substitute for rhododendrons on alkaline soils where bold foliage is required. It will grow into a large shrub. While its flowers are insignificant they release a pungent scent.
Propagation seed, semi-ripe cuttings
Flowering time spring
Size shrub to 8m (26ft)
Pruning after flowering, if necessary
Conditions sun or shade
Propagation hardwood cuttings or seed
Frost hardy/Z 7–8

Elaeagnus spp.
Gumi
Silverberry
Family: Elaeagnaceae
Popular species of elaeagnus include *Elaeagnus pungens, E. glabra* and *E. macrophylla*, but the most common green-leaved form is the hybrid *E. x ebbingei*, with dusty green leaves, which are silvery beneath. In autumn small, creamy-white, bell-shaped flowers are borne in the leaf axils, almost out of sight, but their scent can carry far.

This is a wonderful evergreen for mixed hedges, when it can be pruned to maintain a neat shape, and as a general evergreen backdrop. Variegated forms are available, but are not appropriate for a Japanese garden. The growth of *E. x ebbingei* can be a bit rangy and will need some tidying.
Propagation semi-ripe cuttings
Flowering time autumn
Size shrub to 4m (13ft)
Pruning by cutting back over-long shoots in mid-spring
Conditions full sun or partial shade; any soil
Fully to frost hardy/Z 7–9

Euonymus japonicus
Mayumi
Japanese spindle tree
Family: Celastraceae
A handsome and cheerful evergreen,

Daphniphyllum macropodum

native to Japan, euonymus is often planted in coastal areas owing to its resistance to salt-laden air. It is a variable shrub up to 4m (13ft) tall that has produced many variegated forms, but also a large-leaved variety called 'Macrophyllus' and a dwarf form with minute leaves called 'Microphyllus'. This dwarf form would be suitable for smaller gardens but is on the tender side and may need the shelter of other plants. As with most of this species, *Euonymus japonicus* is easily grown on most soil types. A similar species, *E. fortunei*, is much hardier and has given rise to countless cultivars, many of which, like *E. fortunei* 'Coloratus', can be used as ground cover in dry shady areas.
Propagation hardwood cuttings
Flowering time insignificant
Size shrub to 3m (10ft)
Conditions sun or shade
Pruning in autumn or late winter as a shrub or in midsummer if grown as a hedge
Frost hardy/Z 6–8

OTHER NATIVE JAPANESE EVERGREENS

- *Leucothoe keiskei*, which is a small shrub, to 60cm (24in), with slender, glossy, dark green leaves. It must have acid soil.
- *Nandina domestica* (sacred bamboo; see page 79), which is evergreen in mild areas. It is an upright shrub, to 2m (6½ft), with white flowers in summer and bright red fruit.

Fatsia japonica

Fatsia japonica
Yatsude

Japanese aralia

Family: Araliaceae

Native to the forests of Japan, the Japanese aralia has distinctive large, glossy, divided leaves. The flowers, which resemble those of ivy, are like small explosions; they are initially pale cream-green but turn almost black. A hybrid between *Fatsia* and *Hedera* (ivy), *Fatshedera lizei* (tree ivy), is a rather sprawling but smaller plant, to about 2m (6½ft).

Propagation seed, cuttings
Flowering time autumn
Size shrub to 4m (13ft)
Pruning not needed
Conditions sheltered position in full sun or partial shade; slightly acid, humus-rich soil
Frost hardy/Z 7–9

Ilex crenata

Ilex crenata
Inu tsuge

Japanese bush holly

Family: Aquifoliaceae

The Japanese holly, which can grow up to 6m (20ft) high and as wide, looks more like a box than a holly, especially as its leaves are small and spineless. Like box it can also be clipped into almost any shape. *Ilex crenata* is hardier than both *Buxus sempervirens* and *B. microphyllus*, so could be grown as a substitute for these and azaleas in very cold regions. The species, when unclipped, will grow into a large wide shrub with long narrow leaves, but is highly variable when grown from seed. There are a number of selected forms, such as 'Convexa' with small leaves and a low bushy habit, and 'Helleri' with very small leaves and a dense and flattened habit. The berries are black and not as attractive as those of many holly species.

Propagation seed, semi-ripe cuttings
Flowering time spring
Size shrub to 5m (16ft)
Conditions sun or shade
Propagation hardwood cuttings
Fully hardy/Z 5–8

Ilex integra
Mochi-no-ki

Japanese tree holly

Family: Aquifoliaceae

There are a number of *Ilex* species native to Japan that appear in gardens as part of a general mix of background evergreens. *Ilex integra* (mochi-no-ki) is a large shrub with spineless broad leathery leaves that carries red berries in autumn, while *I. rotunda* (see above right) has rounder leaves. In Western gardens, *Ilex aquifolium* 'J.C. Van Tol' would be a suitable substitute as it also has spineless leaves and red berries. *Ilex x altaclerensis* 'Camelliifolia' is another variety of holly with more rounded and very glossy leaves, reminiscent of camellia foliage, and would make an ideal tall background evergreen for larger gardens. These species and varieties can also be clipped as hedges.

Propagation seed, semi-ripe cuttings
Flowering time spring
Size shrub to 7m (23ft)
Conditions sun or shade
Frost hardy/Z 5–8

Ilex rotunda
Kurogane-mochi

Japanese tree holly

Family: Aquifoliaceae

Propagation seed, semi-ripe cuttings
Flowering time spring
Size tree to 23m (75ft)
Conditions sun or shade
Fully hardy/Z 7–8

Ligustrum japonicum
Nu-zhen-zi

Japanese privet

Family: Oleaceae

A rounded bushy shrub with very shiny and black-green leaves. In late summer and early autumn, like many other privets (if not clipped), it produces pyramidal panicles of small white flowers with a strong, sweet fragrance, which some people find disagreeable. Despite this, the Japanese privet is a useful dense evergreen that in cold areas will need some protection from hard frosts and cold winds. It could form a part of the evergreen mixed plantings used as a background in stroll gardens. *Ligustrum japonica* 'Rotundifolium' has very dense blunt foliage that is thick and leathery, and this is commonly found in Japanese gardens.

Propagation hardwood cuttings
Flowering time summer
Size shrub to 4m (13ft)
Conditions sun or shade
Frost hardy/Z 6–8

TOPIARY AND HEDGES

• Mixed groups of camellias, azaleas, pieris and photinias as well as evergreen oaks and hollies are often clipped into *o-karikomi*, the Japanese equivalent of Western topiary

• These plants can also be grown as hedges. Low hedges of *Camellia sinensis* (tea plant) are often planted in tea gardens; tea plants have much smaller leaves and flowers than the more ornamental camellias and they are less hardy.

Magnolia grandiflora

Taizen-boku

Evergreen magnolia

Family: Magnoliaceae

While this evergreen species of magnolia is native to the USA, it was introduced to Japan by the end of the 19th century and has been extensively planted in gardens. It suits the larger Japanese-style garden due to its bold and glossy foliage. In summer it produces huge creamy white cupped blooms that yield an intoxicating fragrance.

Propagation seed, semi-ripe cuttings, grafted

Flowering time summer

Size tree or large shrub to 10m (30ft)

Pruning best left unpruned; cut back in late winter if necessary

Conditions sun

Frost hardy/Z 7–8

Mahonia japonica

Bealei

Japanese mahonia

Family: Berberidaceae

An erect, pinnate, holly-like plant related to berberis, this mahonia has a strong, architectural shape, and bears spikes of sweetly scented yellow flowers in winter and early spring. When it becomes too woody and overgrown, prune the plant hard, removing the old stems first, immediately after flowering.

Propagation semi-ripe cuttings

Flowering time late autumn to early spring

Size shrub to 2m (6½ft)

Pruning by cutting back over-long shoots after flowering

Conditions sheltered position in partial shade; any reasonable soil

Fully hardy/Z 6–8

Osmanthus fragrans

Mahonia japonica

Osmanthus fragrans

Kinmokusei

Tea olive

Family: Oleaceae

A popular shrub in Japan, the fragrant olive or sweet tea is famed for its creamy autumn flowers, but it is not very hardy. A hardier species, *O. fortunei*, is more suitable for most gardens, or try *O. heterophyllus*, known as hi-ragi, a broad, holly-leaved shrub.

Propagation semi-ripe cuttings

Flowering time autumn

Size shrub to 6m (20ft)

Pruning by cutting back to maintain shape in mid-spring

Conditions sheltered position in sun or partial shade; any reasonable soil

Half hardy/Z 8–9

Photinia glabra

Kaname-mochi

Red-leaf photinia

Family: Rosaceae

Photinias are mostly handsome, broad-leaved evergreen trees and shrubs, often planted to create a backdrop or shade. White flowers are carried in loose panicles from spring to summer, followed by the rosy-red flush of young foliage, evident in hybrids such as 'Red Robin' and 'Birmingham'. Photinias are pretty hardy and can be kept at a manageable height through pruning. They can also be grown as a hedge.

Propagation semi-ripe cuttings

Flowering time late spring to early summer

Size shrub to 5m (16ft)

Pruning by cutting out crossing and badly positioned stems in early spring

Conditions full sun or partial shade; any moist soil

Fully to frost hardy/Z 7–8

Photinia glabra

Pieris japonica

A-sebi

Japanese Andromeda

Family: Ericaceae

A-sebi means "horse-drunk", relating to its poisonous effects on animals. This compact shrub is reasonably hardy, with pendulous clusters of white lily-of-the-valley-like flowers in early spring. The young growth is tinted pink. The Chinese species, *P. formosa*, has brilliant red-bronze young growth but is not as hardy. The American species, *P. floribunda*, is hardy. Pieris prefers acid soil and plenty of humus but can withstand quite dry conditions in late summer. More commonly seen as a large shrub, it can grow into a small tree. Small-leaved and dwarf forms include 'Green Heath', which grows to 60cm (24in).

Propagation seed, semi-ripe cuttings

Flowering time late winter to spring

Size shrub to 3m (10ft)

Pruning remove dead shoots after flowering

Conditions full sun or light shade; acid soil

Fully hardy/Z 6–8

OTHER NON-JAPANESE EVERGREENS

- *Arbutus unedo* (strawberry tree), a spreading small tree or shrub, to 8m (26ft), with creamy white flowers followed by red fruits.
- *Ilex meserveae* (blue holly), a vigorous shrub or small tree, to 5m (16ft), with sharply spined, glossy, blue-green leaves.
- *Prunus lusitanica* (Portugal laurel), a dense shrub or tree, to 20m (66ft), with large, glossy, dark green leaves.

Evergreen trees & conifers

The general Japanese name for conifers is *shohaku-rui*, and the tall, straight pines in particular were said to draw the gods down to Earth, while the Shintoists beat wooden planks to attract them. Such evergreen trees have been regarded in Japan as symbols of chastity, consistency and loyalty. The Hinoki cypress and Japanese cedar are two of Japan's most important timber trees, their naturally resilient wood being used in many of their buildings and garden structures. Two of the native species of pine are the most popular of conifers in Japanese gardens.

Above: Cryptomeria japonica *has a dense habit and thick, spreading branches. The foliage is scaly and finely dissected.*

Cephalotaxus harringtonii

Cephalotaxus harringtonii
Inu-gaya
Japanese plum yew
Family: Cephalotaxaceae
C. h. drupacea is known as the Japanese plum yew or cow's tail pine. It is a medium shrub up to 3m (10ft) high with a dense compact habit. Its short upright needles are quite soft and form a V-shape on the upper side of the branches. As they age, the plant develops into a large mound with elegant drooping branchlets. *C. h.* 'Fastigiata' is quite different with its stiffly upright habit that bears a striking resemblance to the Irish yew.
Propagation seed or hardwood cuttings
Flowering none
Size tree to 10m (30ft)
Conditions sun or part shade
Frost hardy/Z 6–8

Chamaecyparis obtusa
Hinoki
Hinoki cypress
Family: Cupressaceae
Often planted in forests alongside the Japanese cedar, the Hinoki cypress is a valuable timber tree. It is more commonly seen in gardens in its dwarf forms: *C. obtusa* 'Nana Gracilis' grows to 3m (10ft) high and *C. obtusa* 'Pygmaea' reaches only 1.5m (5ft) high. These smaller versions have more character than most cypress-like trees, with their twisted whorls of vivid young growth. Exceptionally hardy, all these plants can tolerate exposed situations. They can also be successfully clipped into hedges and topiary-style (*o-karikomi*) shapes.

Chamaecyparis obtusa

Propagation hardwood cuttings
Size tree to 20m (66ft)
Pruning not needed, but remove dead or diseased branches
Conditions full sun; slightly acid soil
Fully hardy/Z 4–8

SACRED PINES

Pines (*matsu* in Japanese, which means "waiting for a god") were regarded as the king of trees in Japan and are an important image in Japanese poetry. One of the most famous natural Japanese landscapes is Matsushima Bay, in northern Honshu, which is dotted with more than 800 pine-clad islands.

There are few Japanese gardens that do not contain a pine tree. Together with azaleas and maples, they are one of the fundamental ingredients. Many hours of loving care are spent plucking their needles and pruning their boughs, creating shapes that deliberately evoke trees bent by the winds on mountains and seashores. Pine boughs are often draped with decorations for the moon-viewing celebrations, weddings and New Year.

Chamaecyparis pisifera

Chamaecyparis pisifera
Sawara

Sawara cypress
Family: Cupressaceae
This handsome "false cypress" makes a large tree with spreading branches and flattened sprays of dark green foliage. Its main attribute, however, is the number of sports and varieties that have derived from it. The thread cypress, *C. pisifera* 'Filifera', with its long drooping whip-like shoots and broadly shrub-like growth is planted widely in Japanese gardens. In contrast, *C. pisifera* 'Squarrosa' has soft sprays of dark green foliage, and it has a number of dwarf forms such as 'Intermedia' which forms a dense mound of congested bluish foliage. This is an easy tree or shrub to grow in most soil

Cryptomeria japonica

types and will tolerate a certain amount of shade, especially under the canopy of large deciduous trees.
Propagation hardwood cuttings
Flowering none
Size tree to 20m (66ft)
Conditions sun or shade in any well-drained soil
Fully hardy/Zones 4–7

Cryptomeria japonica
Sugi

Japanese cedar
Family: Taxodiaceae
After the pine, the most important and sacred conifer in Japan is the Japanese cedar. This is capable of living for more than 2,000 years and is often planted as a sign of virtue and as a guardian at the entrance of Buddhist and Shinto shrines. Cryptomerias are planted in most of the commercial forests in Japan, as it is an easily worked timber and is used extensively in the building industry. Its aroma makes the wood prized for sake casks. The cryptomeria is a towering, conical tree, with finely dissected, scaly foliage. It is often coppiced in gardens, and the new growth is pruned into tiers with shaped, pompom-like foliage at the ends. It can also be planted on its own or as part of a mixed hedge. There are many cultivated varieties of *C. japonica*, but most are merely curiosities.
Propagation seed, hardwood cuttings
Size tree to 25m (82ft)
Pruning not needed
Conditions full sun or partial shade; deep, moist, slightly acid soil
Fully hardy/Z 6–9

Juniperus chinensis
Ibuki

Chinese juniper
Family: Cupressaceae
The Chinese juniper is a popular subject for clipping into "cloud pruning". It is a highly variable species that has given rise to one particular form, 'Kaizuka', which is popular in Japan and the USA, where it is also called 'Torulosa'. Its unusually angular branches, clothed in dense clusters of bright green foliage, give it a special picturesque outline

Juniperus chinensis

that is ideal for creating a windswept look. *Juniper chinensis* and all its cultivars are very hardy and easy to grow in almost any soil type, even tolerating salt-laden winds, and are best planted in full sun.
Propagation hardwood cuttings
Flowering none
Size tree to 20m (66ft)
Conditions sun
Fully hardy/Z 5–8

Pinus densiflora
Aka-matsu

Japanese red pine
Family: Pinaceae
A fine tree with pinkish-red bark and a rounded head, the Japanese red pine is often pruned to accentuate its soft crown

Pinus densiflora 'Umbraculifera'

Pinus densiflora

Pinus parviflora
Go-yo-matsu

Japanese white pine

Family: Pinaceae

Native to Japan, the Japanese white pine has shorter, grey-green needles and is slower growing and more manageable than either *P. densiflora* or *P. thunbergii*, but it will eventually make a large, multi-stemmed, mounding tree. There are many dwarf forms, including 'Glauca Nana' and 'Hagaromo Seedling', which are suitable for small gardens.

Propagation seed, grafted

Size tree to 20m (66ft)

Pruning needs little pruning to develop a strong structure

Conditions full sun; any well-drained soil

Fully hardy/Z 4–7

Pinus thunbergii
Kuro-matsu

Japanese black pine

Family: Pinaceae

More rugged and darker in leaf and bark than *P. densiflora*, the Japanese black pine is generally pruned into more horizontal and dramatic windswept shapes. It is the most popular pine for bonsai.

Propagation seed, grafted

Size tree to 25m (82ft)

Pruning during the early growing season

Conditions full sun; any well-drained soil

Fully hardy/Z 6–8

Podocarpus macrophyllus

Podocarpus macrophyllus
Kusamaki

Maki

Family: Podocarpaceae

Although most *Podocarpus* species are not very hardy, this one is fully hardy down to -20°C (-4°F). It forms a distinctive shrub or small tree with very long leaves up to 18cm (7in) long, which are bright green above and pale beneath and arranged in dense spirals around the stems. It is grown both in China and Japan as a rather unusual hedge, but is only suited to acid soils. There are many fancy forms of it in Japan, but the straight species is sufficiently interesting to be grown in its own right.

Propagation seed for species and hardwood cuttings for special forms

Flowering none

Size tree to 15m (50ft)

Conditions sun

Half hardy/Z 7-8

and show its elegant, branched structure. *P. densiflora* 'Umbraculifera', known as tanyosho, is a compact, rounded or flat-topped bushy tree, reaching only 2–3m (7–10ft). This dwarf pine can be planted in groves over small hills, giving the impression of a larger landscape.

Propagation seed, grafted

Size tree to 20m (66ft)

Pruning needs little pruning to develop a strong structure

Conditions full sun; any well-drained soil

Fully hardy/Z 3–7

Pinus parviflora

Pinus thunbergii

POPULAR PINES IN JAPANESE GARDENS

- *Pinus densiflora* (red pine)
- *Pinus thunbergii* (black pine)
- *Pinus sylvestris* (Scots pine), especially *P. sylvestris* 'Watereri'
- *Pinus mugo* (dwarf mountain pine), which grows to only 3.5m (11ft) high and is suitable for very small gardens

Sciadopitys verticillata

Sciadopitys verticillata
Koya maki

Japanese umbrella pine

Family: Pinaceae

This is a most distinctive conifer, usually forming a perfect cone shape and retaining its bright green foliage right to the ground. Its most unusual feature is the cool leathery feel to the long pine-like leaves, which stand out from each other like the spokes of an umbrella. It grows very slowly when young, enjoying a moisture-retentive acid soil but tolerating a neutral soil. Although it will grow in light woodland shade, in full sun it is more likely to keep its perfect shape. It is very rare in the wild but in Japan it is found in temple gardens, especially high in the mountains.

Propagation seed for species and hardwood cuttings

Pruning train to maintain a central trunk

Size tree to 20m (66ft)

Conditions sun or part shade

Fully hardy/Z 4–5

Taxus cuspidata
Ichii

Japanese yew

Family: Taxaceae

Taxus cuspidata is hardier than *T. baccata*, the common European yew that is popular for hedging. There are numerous forms of the Japanese yew and hybrids between it and *T. baccata*; some, like 'Hicksii', are quite upright, while others like 'Minima' and 'Nana', which form small dense shrubs, could be planted and clipped in *o-karikomi* style.

Thujopsis dolabrata

Propagation seed or hardwood cuttings

Pruning after growth begins in the spring

Size tree to 15m (50ft)

Conditions sun or part shade

Fully hardy/Z 5–8

Thujopsis dolabrata
Hiba

Japanese elkhorn cypress

Family: Cupressaceae

Thujopsis dolabrata, with its shiny dark green flattened scaly fronds that are silvery on the reverse, is the most interesting of a group of conifers including species of *Thuja*, *Calocedrus* and *Chamaecyparis* that share many similar characteristics. All these evergreens form medium to large trees that are ideal as background planting, for screening or as individual specimens. They all thrive on most soil types and are very hardy. Some have given rise to dwarf forms, such as *Thujopsis dolabrata* 'Nana', which would be more suitable for the smaller garden.

Propagation seed, hardwood cuttings

Pruning bushy forms need no pruning

Size tree to 20m (66ft)

Conditions sun or part shade

Fully hardy/Z 6–8

Tsuga
Tsuga

Hemlock

Family: Pinaceae

A genus of elegant, large trees with fine soft-needled foliage. Although there is a Japanese species, *Tsuga sieboldii* (Southern Japanese hemlock), for gardens there are a number of slow-growing and dwarf forms of the American species, *Tsuga canadensis* (Canadian hemlock). Those with weeping habits such as *Tsuga canadensis* 'Pendula', or smaller dome-shaped varieties such as *Tsuga canadensis* 'Nana', would be very suitable for Japanese gardens.

Propagation hardwood cuttings or grafted

Pruning during the summer

Size tree to 10m (30ft)

Conditions sun or part shade

Fully hardy/Z 4–8

Taxus cuspidata

Tsuga

Ferns

Japanese ferns are regarded as excellent, shapely plants for softening the hard edges of groups of rocks and for providing a sympathetic foil to glossy evergreens, which are planted to give a wooded, wilderness effect around the path in tea gardens. Ferns are often found tucked around the *tsukubai* and other water features, where they can take advantage of the extra moisture. Camellias with light pastel colours and simple plants such as aucubas, nandinas and maples combine well with ferns.

Onoclea sensibilis

Athyrium trichomanes

Ferns vary from the largest tree ferns to tiny species that creep around in crevices, such as *Blechnum penna-marina* (Alpine hard fern). *Athyrium nipponicum pictum* (Japanese painted fern) is native to Japan, and is unique among ferns for its maroon stalk and fronds with a silvery cast. *Athyrium trichomanes* (lady fern) is a finely cut small-leaved fern for tucking into small spaces.

Above: Asplenium scolopendrium, *the hart's-tongue fern, has a distinctive leaf shape.*

Propagation separated by root division
Size from 4–6cm (1½–2½in) to 10m (30ft)
Conditions most species need shade and moisture, and most like humidity
Hardiness dependent on species/Z 4–9

USEFUL NON-JAPANESE FERNS

- *Asplenium scolopendrium* (hart's-tongue fern) has strap-like leaves and thrives in deep shade but must not be allowed to dry out.
- *Dryopteris felix-mas* (robust male fern) and its forms could be used under trees or in gardens which are very dry.

Matteuccia struthiopteris

- *Matteuccia struthiopteris* (ostrich fern), *Onoclea sensibilis* (sensitive fern) and *Osmunda regalis* (flowering fern) are all excellent for ground that is damp or swampy.

Polystichum setiferum

- *Polystichum setiferum* (soft shield fern) is an ideal all-round fern species as it is more or less evergreen. It is best to remove all the old fronds in spring just before the new fronds unfurl. This species will grow in shade and full sun in any reasonable soil as long as it doesn't become too dry. The various forms such as 'Dahlem' with simple plain leaves and 'Herrenhausen' with curly edges to the fronds are excellent for planting along the tea path, and under camellias and aucubas.

Bamboo

Most Japanese gardens are cultivated in temperate climates, where plants such as azaleas, cherries and plums grow well, but in more tropical or subtropical climates it is best to grow plants that are better suited to the heat. However, if you want to create a "tropical look" in a temperate climate, there are various hardy plants that can be used, and bamboo is ideal. Bamboos can be highly invasive plants, so site them carefully. The bamboo species listed below like full sun or partial shade and rich soil, unless stated otherwise.

Above: Pleioblastus humilis *or dwarf bamboo. This fast-growing bamboo makes a good low hedge or screen.*

Pleioblastus humilis
Nakai
Dwarf bamboo
Family: Poaceae
A fairly low-growing bamboo with dark green canes and light green leaves. It can be invasive, so contain the roots.
Propagation division
Size to 1.5m (5ft)
Conditions sheltered in sun or partial shade
Fully to half hardy/Z 1–3

Pleioblastus pygmaeus
Nakai
Pygmy bamboo
Family: Poaceae
This can be planted as ground cover and clipped down to 5–10cm (2–4in) high. It makes a good substitute for lawns or moss.
Size to 40cm (16in)
Conditions semi-shade or full sun
Fully to half hardy/Z 6–11

Pseudosasa japonica

Phyllostachys aurea
Kosan chiku
Fishpole bamboo or golden bamboo
Family: Poaceae
These mid-green canes age to golden-brown. It will spread, so contain the roots.
Propagation division
Size to 10m (33ft)
Conditions moist soil and tolerates drought
Fully to half hardy/Z 6–8

Phyllostachys aureosulcata
Ousou chiku
Yellow-groove bamboo
Family: Poaceae
This has brown-green canes, attractively ribbed with yellow.
Propagation division
Size to 6m (20ft)
Conditions full to partial sun
Fully to half hardy/Z 5–10

Phyllostachys edulis
Kina mousou chiku
Moso bamboo
Family: Poaceae
This evergreen bamboo is often harvested for its huge stems. In colder climates it will not reach its full growth dimensions, which are only seen in the southern half of Japan. *P. edulis heterocycla* has fascinating tortoiseshell-shaped internodes.
Propagation division
Size to 6m (20ft) or more
Conditions Full sun; medium drought tolerance, intolerant of shade
Fully to half hardy/Z 7–11

Phyllostachys nigra
Kuro chiku
Black bamboo
Family: Poaceae
This dramatic bamboo is popular for its polished black stems, especially in the form 'Munro'. The distinctive canes become black with age.
Propagation division
Size to 5m (16ft)
Conditions full sun or partial shade; well-drained soil
Fully to half hardy/Z 7–9

Phyllostachys vivax
Madake
Vivax bamboo or Chinese timber
Family: Poaceae
This makes a good alternative to *P. edulis.*
Size to 25m (82ft)
Conditions full sun to light shade; well-drained soil
Fully to half hardy/Z 6–10

Pseudosasa japonica
Kishima yadake
Arrow bamboo
Family: Poaceae
A tough and rather invasive bamboo with dark green leaves on pale beige stems.
Size to 6m (20ft)
Conditions requires well-drained soil
Fully to half hardy/Z 6–11

Palms

As long as they are grown in sheltered positions, many palms are surprisingly hardy; like bamboos, they can be used for a tropical look in a temperate climate. Their growth is reliable and they are also appealing because they are low-maintenance. Although Japanese gardens tend to be associated more with temperate flora, it is not inappropriate to use palms and other exotic plants, providing that the same design principles are followed. In cold areas, cycads are often wrapped up in winter with straw to protect their leaves and crowns from frost.

Above: Trachycarpus fortunei, *distinctive for its huge fan-shaped leaves, is a very hardy palm and thrives in mild coastal gardens.*

Cycas revoluta
Cycas nana
Sago palm
Family: Cycadaceae
This ancient plant is native to the southern islands of Japan. It is a beautiful glossy evergreen, which looks like a cross between a palm and a fern. It is only marginally hardy, and is rarely seen in gardens north of Kyoto. Even in Kyoto the sago palm has to be wrapped up in winter, and like many other aspects of Japanese gardens, this elaborate wrapping has been raised to the level of an art form.
Propagation seed
Size to 2m (6½ft)
Conditions requires full sun and moist, rich soil.
Frost tender/Z 8–10

Rhapis excelsa
Shuro
Miniature fan palm
Family: Arecaceae/Palmae
Native to China, the miniature fan palm was introduced to Japan in the 19th century. Stockier and spinier than the Chusan palm, but not quite as hardy, it is still a valuable addition to the tropical look in a temperate garden. With shiny dark leaves, the fronds of the miniature fan palm stretch out from an upright furry trunk. The plant can be used as group plantation. It is good for planting in shaded areas.
Propagation sucker division
Size to 5m (16ft)
Conditions requires a sheltered position; light shade and any soil.
Frost tender/Z 8–11

Trachycarpus fortunei
To-juro
Chusan palm
Family: Arecaceae/Palmae
This hardy palm was originally grown for its yield of fibre, and it has since become naturalized in many parts of the country. It grows quite erect and has fan-shaped leaves. Dwarf forms include 'Compacta' and 'Green Pillow'.
Propagation seed
Size full size to 20m (66ft); dwarf forms to 1m (3ft)
Conditions full sun or shade; any soil
Frost hardy/Z 7–10

Cycas revoluta

Trachycarpus fortunei

Other plants of interest

This selection includes plants that can be placed beside the tea path or grown in shady courtyards. Many of them have hundreds of interesting, even quirky, variations, and they are often specially grown in pots so that they can be highlighted. They are not usually grown for planting out in the garden, where they might disrupt the overall scheme. Hollyhocks, popular in English cottage gardens, originated in the Orient, and are often grown against house walls. Mondo grass is the most popular ground cover in Japan, its glossy leaves forming a dense, impenetrable mat.

Above: Farfugium japonicum *is a perennial native to Japan, grown for its attractive foliage and its autumn flowers.*

Alcea rosea

Alcea rosea
Tachia-oi
Hollyhock
Family: Malvaceae
The hollyhock has been popular in Japan since Heian times and is still common, especially in gardens of small houses.
Propagation seed
Flowering time early to midsummer
Size perennial to 2.4m (8ft)
Conditions full sun; any soil
Fully hardy/Z 6–9

Equisetum hyemale
Tokusa
Small tufted mare's tail
Family: Equisetaceae
In Western gardens this is a pernicious but attractive weed that likes wet soils. Japanese forms are less invasive. The vertical, leafless stems of *E. hyemale* are an arresting sight.
Propagation division
Size perennial to 1.5m (5ft)
Conditions sun or partial shade; moist soil
Fully hardy/Z 4–9

Farfugium japonicum
Tsuwa-buki
Leopard plant
Family: Asteraceae/Compositae
The yellow flowers of this evergreen perennial with scalloped leaves are similar to those of *Ligularia*. Many variegated forms have been developed, the most common 'Aureomaculatum', which has random yellow spots on the leaves.
Propagation division
Flowering time autumn to early winter
Size perennial to 60cm (24in)
Conditions partial shade; moist soil
Frost hardy/Z 7–9

Hemerocallis

Hemerocallis
Kisuge or kanzou
Day lily
Family: Hemerocallidaceae
H. fulva is native to Japan and has given rise to hundreds of varieties. In its natural state its flowers are a buff orange, rising up on stalks in summer from a deciduous herbaceous perennial that will colonize large areas in shade or full sun. Day lily flowers last only one day but a succession are produced over several weeks in mid- to late summer. The species *H. flava* produces a lovely fragrance from its yellow flowers in the spring.
Propagation division
Flowering time spring to late summer
Size 90cm (36in)
Conditions sun or shade in most soil types
Fully hardy/Z 4–8

Hosta
Giboshi
Hosta
Family: Hostaceae
Hostas, or plantain lilies, have been planted in Japanese gardens since Heian times. *Hosta sieboldiana*, one of the hostas with the largest leaves, can be seen growing at 1,000m (3,280ft) at the foot of Mount Fuji. *H. plantaginea* has white, scented flowers, while *H. montana* and *H. tardiva*, both native to Japan, are grown for their handsome foliage. *H. ventricosa* is particularly striking,

Hosta

Houttuynia cordata

Lilium

with beautiful violet flowers and strong, green-ribbed foliage. Hostas were selected for their variety of leaf forms during the 19th century. Plants with variegated and twisted leaves were grown as specimens for display, rather than as part of the garden scheme.
Propagation division
Flowering time summer
Size perennial 25–90cm (10–36in)
Conditions sheltered position in sun or partial shade; moist soil
Fully hardy/Z 4–9

Houttuynia cordata
Dokudami
Chameleon houttuynia
Family: Saururaceae
Houttuynia is grown in many Japanese gardens, especially near water, but it can be invasive. The heart-shaped leaves have a strong odour when crushed, while the small white flowers are picked to make herbal tea. There are a number of variegated forms, but the plain green kind is the most popular.
Propagation division
Flowering time spring
Size perennial to 30cm (12in)
Conditions full sun; moist soil
Fully hardy/Z 5–9

Lilium
Yuri
Lily
Family: Liliaceae
Lilium auratum is the golden-rayed lily of Japan. Its large, white, trumpet-like flowers

have freckles and golden streaks inside. It is a fussy plant that needs acid soil with plenty of humus. Hybrids between *L. auratum* and *L. speciosum* are much easier to grow. In Japanese gardens lilies are grown in pots and put out on seasonal display.

The unscented but vibrant *L. lancifolium* (tiger lily), with its orange and yellow, heavily spotted, reflexed flowers, has been grown extensively as a food (where the bulbs are eaten) and is only rarely allowed to flower.
Propagation seed, scales, offsets
Flowering time late summer to early autumn
Size bulb to 1.5m (5ft)
Conditions full sun; acid soil
Frost hardy/Z 4–9

Musa
Musa basjoo
Hardy banana
Family: Musaceae
This will survive frosts as low as -10°C (14°F). Grow it in a sheltered position as its huge leaves tend to get shredded and blackened when exposed to cold winds. In cold areas you can wrap the whole stem up with fleece or straw to protect it in winter. Not really suitable in more "temperate" style gardens, *Musa* could be planted with palms and bamboos for a tropical effect.
Propagation division
Flowering insignificant, may fruit in warm climates
Size shrub to 3m (10ft)
Conditions sun or part shade; sheltered spot
Half hardy/Z 7–9

Ophiopogon japonicus
Ja-no-hige or ryo-no-hige
Japanese mondo grass
Family: Convallariaceae
This leathery, grass-like plant can colonize whole gardens. It has dark green leaves, which curve over. Carpets of it can set off larger plants, such as groups of maples, azaleas and bamboos. The flowers are white or pale blue, followed by small black berries. The dwarf, tufted *O. japonicus* 'Minor' is better in small gardens.
Propagation division
Flowering time summer
Size perennial to 60cm (24in)
Conditions full sun or partial shade; slightly acid soil
Fully hardy/Z 6–10

Ophiopogon japonicus

Index

Above: *Maple leaves at Tenju-an*

PLANT HARDINESS ZONES

Plant entries in the directory of this book have been given hardiness descriptions and zone numbers. Hardiness definitions are as follows:

Fully hardy: A plant which, when planted outside, survives reliably through the winter in the local area. Can withstand temperatures down to −15°C (5°F).

Frost hardy: A plant which, when outside, survives through milder winters in the local area, with additional protection. Withstands temperatures down to −5°C (23°F).

Half hardy: A plant which cannot be grown outside during the colder months in the local area and needs greenhouse protection through the winter. Can withstand temperatures down to 0°C (32°F).

Frost tender: A plant needing heated greenhouse protection through the winter in the local area. May be damaged by temperatures below 5°C (41°F).

There is widespread use of the zone number system to express the hardiness of many plant species and cultivars. The zonal system used, shown below, was developed by the Agricultural Research Service of the United States Department of Agriculture. According to this system, there are 11 zones in total, based on the average annual minimum temperature in a particular geographical zone.

Each plant's zone rating indicates the coldest zone in which a correctly planted subject can survive the winter. Where hardiness is borderline, the first number shows the marginal zone and the second the safer zone.

This is not a hard and fast system, but simply a rough indicator, as many factors other than temperature also play an important part where hardiness is concerned. These factors include altitude, wind exposure, proximity to water, soil type, the presence of snow or shade, night temperature, and the amount of water received by a plant. These kinds of factors can easily alter a plant's hardiness by as much as two zones. The presence of long-term snow cover in the winter especially can allow plants to survive in colder zones.

KEY TO ZONES

Zone 1   Below -45°C (-50°F)
Zone 2   -45 to -40°C (-50 to -40°F)
Zone 3   -40 to -34°C (-40 to -30°F)
Zone 4   -34 to -29°C (-30 to -20°F)
Zone 5   -29 to -23°C (-20 to -10°F)
Zone 6   -23 to -18°C (-10 to 0°F)
Zone 7   -18 to -12°C (0 to 10°F)
Zone 8   -12 to -7°C (10 to 20°F)
Zone 9   -7 to -1°C (20 to 30°F)
Zone 10 -1 to 4°C (30 to 40°F)
Zone 11 Above 4°C (40°F)